1989 Supplement
to
CASES AND MATERIALS
ON
FUNDAMENTALS
OF
CORPORATE TAXATION

By

STEPHEN A. LIND
Professor of Law, University of Florida
and
Hastings College of the Law

STEPHEN SCHWARZ
Professor of Law, Hastings College of the Law

DANIEL J. LATHROPE
Academic Dean and Professor of Law,
Hastings College of the Law

JOSHUA D. ROSENBERG
Professor of Law,
University of San Francisco School of Law

SECOND EDITION

Westbury, New York
THE FOUNDATION PRESS, INC.
1989

KF
6463
.C37
1989
SUPPL.

COPYRIGHT © 1989
By
THE FOUNDATION PRESS, INC.
All rights reserved
ISBN 0–88277–748–3

L., S., L. & R. Corp.Tax. 2nd Ed. UCB
1989 Supp.

PREFACE

Since the second edition of *Fundamentals of Corporate Taxation* was published in June of 1987, the flow of corporate tax developments has slowed but not totally abated. Congress continues to tinker with the Code in its ongoing effort to reduce the deficit, and the Supreme Court's docket over the past two years has included several cases involving corporations and their shareholders.

This Supplement is intended to update the text by summarizing the major cases, regulations, rulings, legislative developments and proposals for additional reforms since 1987, including the Revenue Act of 1987, the Technical and Miscellaneous Revenue Act of 1988, the final Section 355 regulations and the 1989 Congressional hearings on leveraged buyouts and excessive debt.

The Supplement is organized to parallel the main text, with appropriate cross references to chapter headings and page numbers. Developments through April 15, 1989 are covered.

We are indebted to our research assistant, Craig Bergez, for his assistance in preparing the manuscript.

STEPHEN A. LIND
STEPHEN SCHWARZ
DANIEL J. LATHROPE
JOSHUA D. ROSENBERG

San Francisco, California
April, 1989

TABLE OF CONTENTS

[This Table of Contents correlates the Supplement to the Table of Contents in the 1987 edition of *Cases and Materials on Fundamentals of Corporate Taxation*, indicating the pages in the Supplement that contain material supplementing material covered under the listed original headings. Italics indicate new material.]

	Page
PREFACE	iii
TABLE OF INTERNAL REVENUE CODE SECTIONS	ix
TABLE OF TREASURY REGULATIONS	xi
TABLE OF REVENUE RULINGS	xiii
TABLE OF CASES	xv
TABLE OF AUTHORITIES	xvii

PART ONE: INTRODUCTION

Chapter
1. An Overview of the Taxation of Corporations and Shareholders ... 1
   - B. The Corporate Income Tax ... 1
     - 1. Determination of Regular Corporate Tax Liability ... 1
   - C. Classification as a Corporation ... 2
     - 2. Corporations vs. Partnerships ... 2
   - D. Recognition of the Corporate Entity ... 2
   - E. Impact of Corporate Classification ... 9
     - 4. Personal Service Corporations ... 9

PART TWO: TAXATION OF C CORPORATIONS

3. The Capital Structure of a Corporation ... 10
   - B. Debt vs. Equity ... 10
   - D. Character of Loss on Corporate Investment ... 10
     - 2. Loss vs. Contribution to Capital ... 10
4. Nonliquidating Distributions ... 22
   - D. Distributions of Property ... 22
     - 3. Consequences to the Shareholders ... 22
   - F. Anti-Avoidance Limitations on the Dividends Received Deduction ... 22
     - 3. Extraordinary Dividends: Basis Reduction ... 22
     - 5. Section 301(f) ... 23
5. Redemptions and Partial Liquidations ... 24
   - C. Redemptions Tested at the Shareholder Level ... 24
     - 1. Substantially Disproportionate Redemptions ... 24
   - D. Redemptions Tested at the Corporate Level: Partial Liquidations ... 24

v

TABLE OF CONTENTS

Chapter	Page
5. Redemptions and Partial Liquidations—Continued	
E. Consequences to the Distributing Corporation	24
3. Stock Redemption Expenses	24
G. Redemptions Through Related Corporations	25
7. Complete Liquidations and Taxable Dispositions of a Corporation's Assets or Stock	26
B. Complete Liquidations	26
1. Consequences to the Shareholders	26
2. Consequences to the Distributing Corporation	26
c. Limitations on Recognition of Loss	26
3. Liquidation of a Subsidiary	28
b. Consequences to the Distributing Corporation	28
4. Elective One–Month Liquidations	29
C. Taxable Dispositions of a Corporate Business	29
2. Taxable Sales of Corporate Assets	29
c. Transitional Rules	29
5. Selected Planning Considerations	29
c. Special Problems and Opportunities	29
9. Preventing the Improper Retention of Corporate Earnings	31
B. The Accumulated Earnings Tax	31
1. The Proscribed Tax Avoidance Purpose	31
10. Acquisitive Reorganizations	32
B. Types of Acquisitive Reorganizations	32
1. Type A: Statutory Mergers and Consolidations	32
a. Continuity of Interest	32
3. Type C: Acquisitions of Assets for Voting Stock	37
C. Treatment of the Parties to an Acquisitive Reorganization	39
1. Consequences to Shareholders and Security Holders	39
3. Consequences to the Target Corporation	52
11. Nonacquisitive, Nondivisive Reorganizations	57
A. Type E: Recapitalizations	57
3. Use of Recapitalizations in Estate Planning	57
12. Corporate Divisions	58
B. The Requirements for a Tax–Free Corporate Division	58
2. Section 355: In General	58
3. The Active Trade or Business Requirement	58
4. The Device Limitation	63
5. The Judicial Limitations	69
D. The Operative Provisions	73
13. Limitations on Carryovers of Corporate Attributes	75
B. Limitations on Net Operating Loss Carryforwards: Section 382	75
3. Results of an Ownership Change	75

TABLE OF CONTENTS

Chapter	Page
13. Limitations on Carryovers of Corporate Attributes—Continued	
D. Other Loss Limitations	76
1. Acquisitions Made to Evade Tax	76
2. Limitations on Use of Preacquisition Losses to Offset Built-in Gains: Section 384	76
15. The Future of Subchapter C	80
E. Leveraged Buyouts: The Problem of Excessive Debt	80

PART THREE: TAXATION OF S CORPORATIONS

16. The S Corporation	108
C. Election, Revocation and Termination	108
D. Treatment of the Shareholders	109
E. Distributions to Shareholders	110
F. Taxation of the S Corporation	110

*

vii

TABLE OF INTERNAL REVENUE CODE SECTIONS

Sec.	Page	Sec.	Page
11(b)(2)	1	336(d)	26
63(a)	111		27
172	111	336(d)(1)	28
243	65	336(d)(2)	28
	69	336(d)(2)(B)(ii)	26
243(a)(1)	1	336(d)(3)	28
243(a)(3)	1	337	28
243(b)(1)	1		55
243(c)	1	337(a)	28
267(a)(1)	26	337(b)(1)	28
269	76	337(c)	29
	77	338	75
269A(b)(2)	9	338(h)(1)(C)	75
280H	9	351	26
280H(c)	9		53
301	22	355	24
301—307	73		30
301(b)(1)	22		61
301(b)(1)(B)	22		67
301(d)	22		69
301(d)(2)	22		71
301(e)	23		72
301(f) (former)	23		73
302(b)(2)	24	355(a)(1)(B)	63
302(b)(2)(C)	24		65
302(b)(4)	66		66
302(c)(2)(A)(ii)	64	355(a)(3)(A)	73
302(c)(2)(A)(iii)	64	355(b)(2)	30
302(e)	66		61
304	30	355(b)(2)(D)	62
304(a)	30		63
304(b)(4)	25	355(c)	73
	30	357(a)	53
311	73	357(b)	53
	110		54
311(b)	73	357(c)	53
	110		54
312(k)	23	357(c)(1)	53
312(n)	23	358(a)	53
312(n)(7)	23	358(a)(1)	56
332	28	358(a)(2)	54
334(b)(1)	28		55
334(b)(2)	28		56
334(b)(3)	28	358(b)(1)	53
336	73	358(f)	53
	74		54
	110	361	53
336(a)	110		54
336(c)	53		55
	73	361(a)	53
			54

ix

TABLE OF INTERNAL REVENUE CODE SECTIONS

Sec.	Page	Sec.	Page
361(a) (Cont'd)	54	448(d)(2)	1
361(b)(1)(A)	53	453(h)(1)(B)	26
	54	511(a)	28
361(b)(1)(B)	53	531	31
361(b)(2)	53	1001	54
361(b)(3)	54	1031(d)	112
	55	1059	22
361(c)	54	1223(1)	56
361(c)(1)	54	1223(2)	56
	73	1363(d)	110
361(c)(2)	54	1366	109
	73	1371(a)	110
361(c)(3)	54	1374	110
	55		111
361(c)(4)	73		112
362(a)	56	1374(a)	110
362(d)	76	1374(b)(1)	111
368(a)(2)(B)	53	1374(b)(2)	111
368(a)(2)(G)	55	1374(c)(1)	110
382	75	1374(c)(2)	111
	76	1374(d)(1)	111
	77	1374(d)(2)	111
382(e)(2)	75	1374(d)(2)(A)(ii)	111
382(h)(2)(B)	75	1374(d)(2)(B)	111
382(h)(3)(B)	75	1374(d)(3)	111
382(h)(7)	77	1374(d)(4)	111
384	76	1374(d)(6)	112
	77	1374(d)(7)	110
384(a)	77	1374(d)(8)	112
	78	1374(d)(8)(B)	112
384(b)	78	1375(b)(1)(B)	111
384(b)(3)	78	1378(b)(2)	109
384(c)(4)	77	1504(a)(2)	76
384(c)(5)	77	2036(c)	57
384(c)(7)	77	5881	24
384(c)(8)	77	5881(b)	24
384(f)	79	7519	108
388	75		109
444	9	7519(a)(2)	109
	108	7519(b)	109
	109	7519(b)(2)	109
444(a)	108	7519(c)	109
444(b)(1)	108	7519(d)	109
444(b)(2)	9	7519(d)(4)	109
	108	7704	2
444(b)(3)	108	7704(b)	2
444(b)(4)	9	7704(c)	2

x

TABLE OF TREASURY REGULATIONS

Reg.	Page
1.355–1(b)	58
1.355–1(c)(3)	59
1.355–2(a)(5), Ex. (1)	71
1.355–2(a)(5), Ex. (2)	71
1.355–2(b)	69
1.355–2(b)(1)	71
1.355–2(b)(2)	71
1.355–2(b)(3)	71
1.355–2(b)(4)	71
1.355–2(b)(5), Ex. (3)	71
1.355–2(b)(5), Ex. (4)	71
1.355–2(b)(5), Ex. (5)	71
1.355–2(b)(5), Ex. (6)	71
1.355–2(b)(5), Ex. (7)	71
1.355–2(b)(5), Ex. (8)	71
1.355–2(c)	69
1.355–2(c)(1)	71
	72
1.355–2(c)(2), Ex. (2)	72
1.355–2(c)(2), Ex. (3)	72
1.355–2(d)	63
1.355–2(d)(1)	63
	64
1.355–2(d)(2)	65
1.355–2(d)(2)(C)	68
1.355–2(d)(2)(i)	64
	65
1.355–2(d)(2)(ii)	65
1.355–2(d)(2)(iii)(A)	65
1.355–2(d)(2)(iii)(B)	65
1.355–2(d)(2)(iii)(C)	66
1.355–2(d)(2)(iii)(D)	65
	66
1.355–2(d)(2)(iii)(E)	66
1.355–2(d)(2)(iv)	67
1.355–2(d)(2)(iv)(A)	67
1.355–2(d)(2)(iv)(B)	67
1.355–2(d)(2)(iv)(C)	60
	62

Reg.	Page
1.355–2(d)(3)	65
1.355–2(d)(3)(C)	68
1.355–2(d)(3)(i)	64
	65
1.355–2(d)(3)(ii)	68
	71
1.355–2(d)(3)(iii)	68
1.355–2(d)(3)(iv)	69
1.355–2(d)(4), Ex. (2)	67
1.355–2(d)(4), Ex. (3)	67
1.355–2(d)(5)(i)	64
1.355–2(d)(5)(ii)	64
1.355–2(d)(5)(iii)	64
1.355–2(d)(5)(iv)	64
1.355–2(d)(5)(v), Ex. (2)	64
1.355–3	24
	58
1.355–3(b)(2)(ii)	58
	59
1.355–3(b)(2)(iii)	59
1.355–3(b)(2)(iv)	59
	61
	62
1.355–3(b)(3)(ii)	61
1.355–3(c), Ex. (2)	62
1.355–3(c), Ex. (3)	62
1.355–3(c), Ex. (4)	59
1.355–3(c), Ex. (5)	59
1.355–3(c), Ex. (7)	61
1.355–3(c), Ex. (8)	61
1.355–3(c), Ex. (9)	59
1.355–3(c), Ex. (10)	60
1.355–3(c), Ex. (11)	60
	68
1.355–3(c), Ex. (12)	62
1.355–3(c), Ex. (13)	62
1.357–1(a)	53
1.1502–34	29

TABLE OF REVENUE RULINGS
Rulings with accompanying text are indicated by italic type

REVENUE PROCEDURE

Rev.Proc.	Page
88–48	*37*

REVENUE RULINGS

Rev.Rul.	Page
56–451	61
56–655	61
59–400	61
71–383	63

REVENUE RULINGS

Rev.Rul.	Page
72–327	54
74–5	62
75–223	66
76–187	71
79–273	72
87–88	24
88–34	*69*

TABLE OF CASES

Principal cases are in italic type. Non-principal cases are in roman type. References are to Pages.

Bollinger, Commissioner v., 2
Clark, Commissioner v., 39
Coady v. Commissioner, 59
Commissioner v. ___ (see opposing party)

Esmark, Inc. v. Commissioner, 32, 32
Estate of (see name of party)

Fec Liquidating Corp. v. United States, 55
Fink, Commissioner v., 10

General Housewares Corp. v. United States, 55

Leavitt, Estate of v. Commissioner, 109
Lockwood's Estate v. Commissioner, 58, 60, 61

Marett, United States v., 59
Morgenstern v. Commissioner, 67

United States v. ___ (see opposing party)

TABLE OF AUTHORITIES

Authorities with accompanying text are indicated by italic type

Eustice, "A Case Study in Technical Tax Reform: Section 361, or How Not to Revise a Statute," 35 Tax Notes 283 (April 20, 1987), 54

Joint Committee on Taxation, Federal Income Tax Aspects of Corporate Financial Structures, 101st Cong., 1st Sess. (JCS 1-89, Jan. 18, 1989), 80

Staff of Joint Committee on Taxation, Description of Technical Corrections Bill of 1988, 100th Cong., 2d Sess. 386 (1988), 73

Staff of Joint Committee on Taxation, Description of the Technical Corrections Act of 1988 (H.R. 4333 and S. 2238), 100th Cong., 2d Sess. 55–56 (1988), 27

Staff of Joint Committee on Taxation, Description of the Technical Corrections Bill of 1988, 100th Cong., 2d Sess. 421 (1988), 77

Staff of Joint Committee on Taxation, General Explanation of the Tax Reform Act of 1986, 100th Cong., 1st Sess. 341–346 (1987), 27

Yin, "Taxing Corporate Liquidations (and Related Matters) After the Tax Reform Act of 1986," 42 Tax L.Rev. 573 (1987), 27

*

1989 Supplement to CASES AND MATERIALS ON FUNDAMENTALS OF CORPORATE TAXATION

*

PART ONE: INTRODUCTION

CHAPTER 1. AN OVERVIEW OF THE TAXATION OF CORPORATIONS AND SHAREHOLDERS

B. THE CORPORATE INCOME TAX

Page 7:

After the third full paragraph, insert:

In an effort to prevent service businesses from taking what little advantage was left of the lower corporate rates on taxable income below $75,000, the Revenue Act of 1987 (hereafter referred to as "the 1987 Act") added Section 11(b)(2), which denies the benefit of the 15 percent and 25 percent graduated rates to any "qualified personal service corporation," as defined in Section 448(d)(2). Incorporated service businesses thus will be subject to a 34 percent flat rate tax on all their taxable income, effective for taxable years beginning after December 31, 1987. In general, a "qualified personal service corporation" is a corporation substantially engaged in the performance of services in the fields of health, law, engineering, architecture, accounting, actuarial science, performing arts, or consulting, if substantially all of the corporation's stock is held (directly or indirectly) by employees performing services for the corporation, retired employees or the estates of employees or retired employees. § 448(d)(2).

Page 8:

After the last full paragraph, add:

The 1987 Act reduced the Section 243(a)(1) dividends received deduction from 80 percent to 70 percent, effective for dividends received or accrued after December 31, 1987. The reduction applies to corporate shareholders that own less than 20 percent of the stock (measured by vote and value) of the distributing corporation. Corporations owning at least 20 percent but less than 80 percent of the stock of a distributing corporation are still entitled to the 80 percent dividends received deduction. § 243(c). Corporations owning 80 percent or more of the distributing corporation's stock continue to be eligible for a 100 percent dividends received deduction under certain conditions, including an election by all members of the affiliated group covering a variety of tax items beyond the dividends received deduction. § 243(a)(3), (b)(1).

C. CLASSIFICATION AS A CORPORATION

Page 19:

After the carryover paragraph, add:

In the 1987 Act, Congress promptly reacted to the disincorporation threat by enacting Section 7704, which treats certain "publicly traded partnerships" as corporations for tax purposes. A "publicly traded partnership" ("PTP") is any partnership whose interests are: (1) traded on an established securities market, or (2) readily tradable on a secondary market (or its substantial equivalent). § 7704(b). An exception (allowing a PTP to continue to be taxed as a partnership) is provided if 90 percent or more of the partnership's gross income consists of certain passive investment income items (e.g., interest, dividends, real property rents, gains from the sale of real property and income and gains from certain natural resources activities). § 7704(c). Transitional relief, in the form of a ten year delay in reclassification, was provided for certain partnerships that were publicly traded (or had an S.E.C. registration pending) on December 17, 1987. 1987 Act, § 10211(c).

Congress also directed the Treasury to conduct a study of publicly traded partnerships, "including the issues of disincorporation and opportunities for avoidance of the corporate tax" and related administrative and compliance issues related to large partnerships, and to report back to the Congressional tax-writing committees not later than January 1, 1989. 1987 Act, § 10215. At this writing (April, 1989), we await the report.

For the Service's guidance on the definition of a publicly traded partnership, see I.R.S. Notice 88–75, I.R.B. 1988–27, 29.

D. RECOGNITION OF THE CORPORATE ENTITY

Page 46:

Delete the Frink case and insert:

COMMISSIONER v. BOLLINGER

Supreme Court of the United States, 1988.
485 U.S. 340, 108 S.Ct. 1173.

Justice SCALIA delivered the opinion of the Court.

Petitioner the Commissioner of Internal Revenue challenges a decision by the United States Court of Appeals for the Sixth Circuit holding that a corporation which held record title to real property as agent for the corporation's shareholders was not the owner of the property for purposes of federal income taxation. 807 F.2d 65 (1986). We granted certiorari, 482 U.S. 913, 107 S.Ct. 3183, 96 L.Ed.2d 672 (1987), to resolve a conflict in the courts of appeals over the tax treatment of corporations purporting to be agents for their shareholders. * * *

I

Respondent Jesse C. Bollinger, Jr., developed, either individually or in partnership with some or all of the other respondents, eight apartment complexes in Lexington, Kentucky. (For convenience we will refer to all the ventures as "partnerships.") Bollinger initiated development of the first apartment complex, Creekside North Apartments, in 1968. The Massachusetts Mutual Life Insurance Company agreed to provide permanent financing by lending $1,075,000 to "the corporate nominee of Jesse C. Bollinger, Jr." at an annual interest rate of eight percent, secured by a mortgage on the property and a personal guaranty from Bollinger. The loan commitment was structured in this fashion because Kentucky's usury law at the time limited the annual interest rate for noncorporate borrowers to seven percent. Ky.Rev. Stat. §§ 360.010, 360.025 (1972). Lenders willing to provide money only at higher rates required the nominal debtor and record title holder of mortgaged property to be a corporate nominee of the true owner and borrower. On October 14, 1968, Bollinger incorporated Creekside, Inc., under the laws of Kentucky; he was the only stockholder. The next day, Bollinger and Creekside, Inc., entered into a written agreement which provided that the corporation would hold title to the apartment complex as Bollinger's agent for the sole purpose of securing financing, and would convey, assign, or encumber the property and disburse the proceeds thereof only as directed by Bollinger; that Creekside, Inc., had no obligation to maintain the property or assume any liability by reason of the execution of promissory notes or otherwise; and that Bollinger would indemnify and hold the corporation harmless from any liability it might sustain as his agent and nominee.

Having secured the commitment for permanent financing, Bollinger, acting through Creekside, Inc., borrowed the construction funds for the apartment complex from Citizens Fidelity Bank and Trust Company. Creekside, Inc., executed all necessary loan documents including the promissory note and mortgage, and transferred all loan proceeds to Bollinger's individual construction account. Bollinger acted as general contractor for the construction, hired the necessary employees, and paid the expenses out of the construction account. When construction was completed, Bollinger obtained, again through Creekside, Inc., permanent financing from Massachusetts Mutual Life in accordance with the earlier loan commitment. These loan proceeds were used to pay off the Citizens Fidelity construction loan. Bollinger hired a resident manager to rent the apartments, execute leases with tenants, collect and deposit the rents, and maintain operating records. The manager deposited all rental receipts into, and paid all operating expenses from, an operating account, which was first opened in the name of Creekside, Inc., but was later changed to "Creekside Apartments, a partnership." The operation of Creekside North Apartments generated losses for the taxable years 1969, 1971, 1972, 1973, and 1974, and ordinary income for the years 1970, 1975, 1976, and 1977. Throughout, the income and losses were reported by Bollinger on his individual income tax returns.

Following a substantially identical pattern, seven other apartment complexes were developed by respondents through seven separate partnerships. For each venture, a partnership executed a nominee agreement with Creekside, Inc., to obtain financing. (For one of the ventures, a different Kentucky corporation, Cloisters, Inc., in which Bollinger had a 50 percent interest, acted as the borrower and titleholder. For convenience, we will refer to both Creekside and Cloisters as "the corporation.") The corporation transferred the construction loan proceeds to the partnership's construction account, and the partnership hired a construction supervisor who oversaw construction. Upon completion of construction, each partnership actively managed its apartment complex, depositing all rental receipts into, and paying all expenses from, a separate partnership account for each apartment complex. The corporation had no assets, liabilities, employees, or bank accounts. In every case, the lenders regarded the partnership as the owner of the apartments and were aware that the corporation was acting as agent of the partnership in holding record title. The partnerships reported the income and losses generated by the apartment complexes on their partnership tax returns, and respondents reported their distributive share of the partnership income and losses on their individual tax returns.

The Commissioner of Internal Revenue disallowed the losses reported by respondents, on the ground that the standards set out in National Carbide Corp. v. Commissioner, 336 U.S. 422, 69 S.Ct. 726, 93 L.Ed. 779 (1949), were not met. The Commissioner contended that *National Carbide* required a corporation to have an arm's-length relationship with its shareholders before it could be recognized as their agent. Although not all respondents were shareholders of the corporation, the Commissioner took the position that the funds the partnerships disbursed to pay expenses should be deemed contributions to the corporation's capital, thereby making all respondents constructive stockholders. Since, in the Commissioner's view, the corporation rather than its shareholders owned the real estate, any losses sustained by the ventures were attributable to the corporation and not respondents. Respondents sought a redetermination in the United States Tax Court. The Tax Court held that the corporations were the agents of the partnerships and should be disregarded for tax purposes. Bollinger v. Commissioner, 48 TCM 1443 (1984), ¶ 84, 560 P-H Memo TC. On appeal, the United States Court of Appeals for the Sixth Circuit affirmed. 807 F.2d 65 (1986). We granted the Commissioner's petition for certiorari.

II

For federal income tax purposes, gain or loss from the sale or use of property is attributable to the owner of the property. See Helvering v. Horst, 311 U.S. 112, 116–117, 61 S.Ct. 144, 147, 85 L.Ed. 75 (1940); Blair v. Commissioner, 300 U.S. 5, 12, 57 S.Ct. 330, 333, 81 L.Ed. 465 (1937); see also Commissioner v. Sunnen, 333 U.S. 591, 604, 68 S.Ct. 715, 722, 92 L.Ed. 898 (1948). The problem we face here is that two different taxpayers can plausibly be regarded as the owner. Neither the Internal Revenue Code nor the regulations promulgated by the Secretary of the Treasury provide significant guidance as to which should be selected. It is common ground between the parties, however, that if a corporation holds title to property as agent for a partnership, then for tax purposes the partnership and not the corporation is the owner. Given agreement on that premise, one would suppose that there would be agreement upon the conclusion as well. For each of respondents' apartment complexes, an agency agreement expressly provided that the corporation would "hold such property as nominee and agent for" the partnership, App. to Pet. for Cert. 21a, n. 4, and that the partnership would have sole control of and responsibility for the apartment complex. The partnership in each instance was identified as the principal and owner of the property during financing, construction, and operation. The lenders, contractors, managers, employees, and tenants—all who had contact with the development—knew that the corporation was merely the agent of the partnership, if they knew of the existence of the corporation at all. In each instance the relationship between the corporation and the partnership was, in both form and substance, an agency with the partnership as principal.

The Commissioner contends, however, that the normal indicia of agency cannot suffice for tax purposes when, as here, the alleged principals are the controlling shareholders of the alleged agent corporation. That, it asserts, would undermine the principle of Moline Properties v. Commissioner, 319 U.S. 436, 63 S.Ct. 1132, 87 L.Ed. 1499 (1943), which held that a corporation is a separate taxable entity even if it has only one shareholder who exercises total control over its affairs. Obviously, *Moline's* separate-entity principle would be significantly compromised if shareholders of closely held corporations could, by clothing the corporation with some attributes of agency with respect to particular assets, leave themselves free at the end of the tax year to make a claim—perhaps even a good-faith claim—of either agent or owner status, depending upon which choice turns out to minimize their tax liability. The Commissioner does not have the resources to audit and litigate the many cases in which agency status could be thought debatable. Hence, the Commissioner argues, in this shareholder context he can reasonably demand that the taxpayer meet a prophylactically clear test of agency.

We agree with that principle, but the question remains whether the test the Commissioner proposes is appropriate. The parties have debated at length the significance of our opinion in National Carbide Corp. v. Commissioner, supra. In that case, three corporations that were wholly owned subsidiaries of another corporation agreed to operate their production plants as "agents" for the parent, transferring to it all profits except for a nominal sum. The subsidiaries reported as gross income only this sum, but the Commissioner concluded that they should be taxed on the entirety of the profits because they were not really agents. We agreed, reasoning first, that the mere fact of the parent's control over the subsidiaries did not establish the existence of an agency, since such control is typical of all shareholder-corporation relationships, id., 336 U.S. at 429–434, 69 S.Ct., at 730–732; and second, that the agreements to pay the parent all profits above a nominal amount were not determinative since income must be taxed to those who actually earn it without regard to anticipatory assignment, id., at 435–436, 69 S.Ct., at 733–734. We acknowledged, however, that there was such a thing as "a true corporate agent ... of [an] owner-principal," id., at 437, 69 S.Ct., at 734, and proceeded to set forth four indicia and two requirements of such status, the sum of which has become known in the lore of federal income tax law as the "six *National Carbide* factors":

> "[1] Whether the corporation operates in the name and for the account of the principal, [2] binds the principal by its actions, [3] transmits money received to the principal, and [4] whether receipt of income is attributable to the services of employees of the principal and to assets belonging to the principal are some of the relevant considerations in determining whether a true agency exists. [5] If the corporation is a true agent, its relations with its principal must not be dependent upon the fact that it is owned by the principal, if such is the case. [6] Its business purpose must be the carrying on of the normal duties of an agent." Id., at 437, 69 S.Ct., at 734 (footnotes omitted).

We readily discerned that these factors led to a conclusion of nonagency in *National Carbide* itself. There each subsidiary had represented to its customers that it (not the parent) was the company manufacturing and selling its products; each had sought to shield the parent from service of legal process; and the operations had used thousands of the subsidiaries' employees and nearly $20 million worth of property and equipment listed as assets on the subsidiaries' books. Id., at 425, 434, 438, and n. 21, 69 S.Ct., at 728, 732–733, 734, and n. 21.

The Commissioner contends that the last two *National Carbide* factors are not satisfied in the present case. To take the last first: The Commissioner argues that here the corporation's business purpose with respect to the property at issue was not "the carrying on of the normal duties of an agent," since it was acting not as the agent but rather as the owner of the property for purposes of Kentucky's usury laws. We do not agree. It assuredly was not acting as the owner in fact, since respondents represented themselves as the principals to all parties concerned with the loans. Indeed, it was the lenders themselves who required the use of a corporate nominee. Nor does it make any sense to adopt a contrary-to-fact legal presumption that the corporation was the principal, imposing a federal tax sanction for the apparent evasion of Kentucky's usury law. To begin with, the Commissioner has not established that these transactions were an evasion. Respondents assert without contradiction that use of agency arrangements in order to permit higher interest was common practice, and it is by no means clear that the practice violated the spirit of the Kentucky law, much less its letter. It might well be thought that the borrower does not generally require usury protection in a transaction sophisticated enough to employ a corporate agent—assuredly not the normal *modus operandi* of the loan shark. That the statute positively envisioned corporate nominees is suggested by a provision which forbids charging the higher corporate interest rates "to a corporation, the principal asset of which shall be the ownership of a one (1) or two (2) family dwelling." Ky.Rev.Stat. § 360.025(2) (1987)—which would seem to prevent use of the nominee device for ordinary home-mortgage loans. In any event, even if the transaction did run afoul of the usury law, Kentucky, like most States, regards only the lender as the usurer, and the borrower as the victim. See Ky.Rev.Stat. § 360.020 (1987) (lender liable to borrower for civil penalty), § 360.990 (lender guilty of misdemeanor). Since the Kentucky statute imposed no penalties upon the borrower for allowing himself to be victimized, nor treated him as *in pari delictu*, but to the contrary enabled him to pay back the principal without any interest, and to sue for double the amount of interest already paid (plus attorney's fees), see Ky.Rev.Stat. § 360.020 (1972), the United States would hardly be vindicating Kentucky law by depriving the usury victim of tax advantages he would otherwise enjoy. In sum, we see no basis in either fact or policy for holding that the corporation was the principal because of the nature of its participation in the loans.

Of more general importance is the Commissioner's contention that the arrangements here violate the fifth *National Carbide* factor—that the corporate agent's "relations with its principal must not be dependent upon the fact that it is owned by the principal." The Commissioner asserts that this cannot be satisfied unless the corporate agent and its shareholder principal have an "arm's-length relationship" that includes the payment of a fee for agency services. The meaning of *National Carbide*'s fifth factor is, at the risk of understatement, not entirely clear. Ultimately, the relations between a corporate agent and its owner-principal are *always* dependent upon the fact of ownership, in that the owner can cause the relations to be altered or terminated at any time. Plainly that is not what was meant, since on that interpretation all subsidiary-parent agencies would be invalid for tax purposes, a position which the *National Carbide* opinion specifically disavowed. We think the fifth *National Carbide* factor—so much more abstract than the others—was no more and no less than a generalized statement of the concern, expressed earlier in our own discussion, that the separate-entity doctrine of *Moline* not be subverted.

In any case, we decline to parse the text of *National Carbide* as though that were itself the governing statute. As noted earlier, it is uncontested that the law attributes tax consequences of property held by a genuine agent to the principal; and we agree that it is reasonable for the Commissioner to demand unequivocal evidence of genuineness in the corporation-shareholder context, in order to prevent evasion of *Moline*. We see no basis, however, for holding that unequivocal evidence can only consist of the rigid requirements (arm's-length dealing plus agency fee) that the Commissioner suggests. Neither of those is demanded by the law of agency, which permits agents to be unpaid family members, friends, or associates. See Restatement (Second) of Agency §§ 16, 21, 22 (1958). It seems to us that the genuineness of the agency relationship is adequately assured, and tax-avoiding manipulation adequately avoided, when the fact that the corporation is acting as agent for its shareholders with respect to a particular asset is set forth in a written agreement at the time the asset is acquired, the corporation functions as agent and not principal with respect to the asset for all purposes, and the corporation is held out as the agent and not principal in all dealings with third parties relating to the asset. Since these requirements were met here, the judgment of the Court of Appeals is

Affirmed.

Justice KENNEDY took no part in the consideration or decision of this case.

Ch. 1   *TAXATION OF CORPORATIONS & SHAREHOLDERS*

E. IMPACT OF CORPORATE CLASSIFICATION

Page 56:

After the second full paragraph, add:

In the 1987 Act, Congress relented somewhat on the taxable year requirements for personal service corporations. (Similar relief was provided for S corporations and partnerships; see infra this Supplement, page 108.) Effective for taxable years beginning after 1986, a personal service corporation which otherwise would have been required to change to a calendar year may elect under new Section 444 to adopt or change to a fiscal year with a "deferral period" (see § 444(b)(4)) of not more than three months. § 444(b)(2). The "deferral period" of a taxable year is the number of months between the beginning of the taxable year elected and the close of the required taxable year that ends within the taxable year elected. Thus, if a corporation otherwise required to use a calendar year elects a fiscal year ending October 31, the deferral period would be two months—the number of months between November 1 (the beginning of the fiscal year) and December 31 (the close of the required taxable year ending within the elected fiscal year). Because personal service corporations ordinarily must use a calendar year, Section 444 thus would permit such corporations to elect a tax year ending September 30, October 31 or November 30.

Congress was aware of the tax deferral benefits resulting from fiscal years. To achieve a rough payback of these deferral benefits, personal service corporations making a Section 444 election are subject to new Section 280H, which generally requires electing corporations to make certain minimum distributions to "employee-owners" (as defined in Section 269A(b)(2)) during the portion of its fiscal year that ends on December 31. If these minimum distribution requirements are not met, the electing corporation may be required to defer certain otherwise currently deductible payments (e.g., compensation) to employee-owners. § 280H(c).

A personal service corporation that establishes a business purpose for a fiscal year is not required to make a Section 444 election and will not be subject to the deduction limitations and distribution requirements in § 280H. I.R.S. Notice 88–10, 1988-1 C.B. 478.

PART TWO: TAXATION OF C CORPORATIONS

CHAPTER 3. THE CAPITAL STRUCTURE OF A CORPORATION

B. DEBT VS. EQUITY

Page 113:

After the case, add:

NOTE

In recent years, corporations have engaged in a number of restructuring transactions which result in the replacement of corporate equity with debt. These include leveraged buyouts, debt-for-equity swaps, corporate repurchases of stock and leveraged employee stock ownership plans. The shift from equity to debt has provoked Congress to revisit various proposals which would reduce the tax bias toward debt. Excerpts from a 1989 Congressional staff report addressing the perceived problems and possible cures are included infra, this Supplement, pages 80–107.

D. CHARACTER OF LOSS ON CORPORATE INVESTMENT

Page 127:

Delete the Frantz case and insert:

COMMISSIONER v. FINK
Supreme Court of the United States, 1987.
483 U.S. 89, 107 S.Ct. 2729.

Justice POWELL delivered the opinion of the Court.

The question in this case is whether a dominant shareholder who voluntarily surrenders a portion of his shares to the corporation, but retains control, may immediately deduct from taxable income his basis in the surrendered shares.

I

Respondents Peter and Karla Fink were the principal shareholders of Travco Corporation, a Michigan manufacturer of motor homes. Travco had one class of common stock outstanding and no preferred stock. Mr. Fink owned 52.2 percent, and Mrs. Fink 20.3 percent, of the

Ch. 3   CAPITAL STRUCTURE OF A CORPORATION

outstanding shares.¹ Travco urgently needed new capital as a result of financial difficulties it encountered in the mid–1970s. The Finks voluntarily surrendered some of their shares to Travco in an effort to "increase the attractiveness of the corporation to outside investors." * * * Mr. Fink surrendered 116,146 shares in December 1976; Mrs. Fink surrendered 80,000 shares in January 1977. As a result, the Finks' combined percentage ownership of Travco was reduced from 72.5 percent to 68.5 percent. The Finks received no consideration for the surrendered shares, and no other shareholder surrendered any stock. The effort to attract new investors was unsuccessful, and the corporation eventually was liquidated.

On their 1976 and 1977 joint federal income tax returns, the Finks claimed ordinary loss deductions totaling $389,040, the full amount of their adjusted basis in the surrendered shares.² The Commissioner of Internal Revenue disallowed the deductions. He concluded that the stock surrendered was a contribution to the corporation's capital. Accordingly, the Commissioner determined that the surrender resulted in no immediate tax consequences, and that the Finks' basis in the surrendered shares should be added to the basis of their remaining shares of Travco stock.

In an unpublished opinion, the Tax Court sustained the Commissioner's determination for the reasons stated in Frantz v. Commissioner, 83 T.C. 162, 174–182 (1984), aff'd, 784 F.2d 119 (CA2 1986), cert. pending, No. 86–11. In *Frantz* the Tax Court held that a stockholder's non pro rata surrender of shares to the corporation does not produce an immediate loss. The court reasoned that "[t]his conclusion ... necessarily follows from a recognition of the purpose of the transfer, that is, to bolster the financial position of [the corporation] and, hence, to protect and make more valuable [the stockholder's] retained shares." 83 T.C., at 181. Because the purpose of the shareholder's surrender is "to decrease or avoid a loss on his overall investment," the Tax Court in *Frantz* was "unable to conclude that [he] sustained a loss at the time of the transaction." Ibid. "Whether [the shareholder] would sustain a loss, and if so, the amount thereof, could only be determined when he subsequently disposed of the stock that the surrender was intended to protect and make more valuable." Ibid. The Tax Court recognized that it had sustained the taxpayer's position in a series of prior cases.³

---

1. In addition, Mr. Fink's sister owned 10 percent of the stock, his brother-in-law owned 4.1 percent, and his mother owned 2.2 percent. App. to Pet. for Cert. 30a.

2. The unadjusted basis of shares is their cost. 26 U.S.C. § 1012. Adjustments to basis are made for, among other things, "expenditures, receipts, losses, or other items, properly chargeable to capital account." § 1016(a)(1).

3. *E.g.*, Tilford v. Commissioner, 75 T.C. 134 (1980), rev'd, 705 F.2d 828 (CA6), cert. denied, 464 U.S. 992, 104 S.Ct. 485, 78 L.Ed.2d 681 (1983); Smith v. Commissioner, 66 T.C. 622, 648 (1976), rev'd sub nom. Schleppy v. Commissioner, 601 F.2d 196

Id., at 174–175. But it concluded that these decisions were incorrect, in part because they "encourage[d] a conversion of eventual capital losses into immediate ordinary losses." Id., at 182.[4]

In this case, a divided panel of the Court of Appeals for the Sixth Circuit reversed the Tax Court. 789 F.2d 427 (1986). The court concluded that the proper tax treatment of this type of stock surrender turns on the choice between "unitary" and "fragmented" views of stock ownership. Under the "'fragmented view,'" "each share of stock is considered a separate investment," and gain or loss is computed separately on the sale or other disposition of each share. Id., at 429. According to the "'unitary view,'" "the 'stockholder's entire investment is viewed as a single indivisible property unit,'" ibid. (citation omitted), and a sale or disposition of some of the stockholder's shares only produces "an ascertainable gain or loss when the stockholder has disposed of his remaining shares." Id., at 432. The court observed that both it and the Tax Court generally had adhered to the fragmented view, and concluded that "the facts of the instant case [do not] present sufficient justification for abandoning" it. Id., at 431. It therefore held that the Finks were entitled to deduct their basis in the surrendered shares immediately as an ordinary loss, except to the extent that the surrender had increased the value of their remaining shares. The Court of Appeals remanded the case to the Tax Court for a determination of the increase, if any, in the value of the Finks' remaining shares that was attributable to the surrender.

Judge Joiner dissented. Because the taxpayers' "sole motivation in disposing of certain shares is to benefit the other shares they hold[,]

(CA5 1979); Downer v. Commissioner, 48 T.C. 86, 91 (1967); Estate of Foster v. Commissioner, 9 T.C. 930, 934 (1947); Miller v. Commissioner, 45 B.T.A. 292, 299 (1941); Budd International Corp. v. Commissioner, 45 B.T.A. 737, 755–756 (1941). The Commissioner acquiesced in *Miller* and *Budd,* but later withdrew his acquiescence. See 1941–2 C.B. 9, 1942–2 C.B. 3; 1977–1 C.B. 2.

The dissent overstates the extent to which the Commissioner's disallowance of ordinary loss deductions is contrary to the "settled construction of law." Post, at 2738. In fact, the Commissioner's position was uncertain when the Finks surrendered their shares in 1976 and 1977. Although the Commissioner had acquiesced in the Tax Court's holdings that non pro rata surrenders give rise to ordinary losses, "it often took a contrary position in litigation." Note, Frantz or Fink: Unitary or Fractional View for Non–Prorata Stock Surrenders, 48 U.Pitt.L.Rev. 905, 908 (1987). See, e.g., Smith v. Commissioner, supra, at 647–650; Duell v. Commissioner, 19 T.C.M. (CCH) 1381 (1960). In 1969, moreover, the Commissioner clearly took the position that a non pro rata surrender by a majority shareholder is a contribution to capital that does not result in an immediate loss. Rev.Rul. 69–368, 1969–2 C.B. 27. Thus, the Finks, unlike the taxpayer in Dickman v. Commissioner, 465 U.S. 330, 104 S.Ct. 1086, 79 L.Ed.2d 343 (1984), knew or should have known that their ordinary loss deductions might not be allowed. For this reason, the Commissioner's disallowance of the Finks' deductions was not an abuse of discretion.

4. The Court of Appeals for the Second Circuit affirmed the Tax Court's holding and agreed with its reasoning. Frantz v. Commissioner, 784 F.2d 119, 123–126 (1986), cert. pending. No. 86–11.

Ch. 3   CAPITAL STRUCTURE OF A CORPORATION

* * * [v]iewing the surrender of each share as the termination of an individual investment ignores the very reason for the surrender." Id., at 435. He concluded: "Particularly in cases such as this, where the diminution in the shareholder's corporate control and equity interest is so minute as to be illusory, the stock surrender should be regarded as a contribution to capital." Ibid.

We granted certiorari to resolve a conflict among the circuits,[5] 479 U.S. 960, 107 S.Ct. 454, 93 L.Ed.2d 401 (1986), and now reverse.

II

A

It is settled that a shareholder's voluntary contribution to the capital of the corporation has no immediate tax consequences. 26 U.S.C. § 263; 26 CFR § 1.263(a)–2(f) (1986). Instead, the shareholder is entitled to increase the basis of his shares by the amount of his basis in the property transferred to the corporation. See 26 U.S.C. § 1016(a)(1). When the shareholder later disposes of his shares, his contribution is reflected as a smaller taxable gain or a larger deductible loss. This rule applies not only to transfers of cash or tangible property, but also to a shareholder's forgiveness of a debt owed to him by the corporation. 26 CFR § 1.61–12(a) (1986). Such transfers are treated as contributions to capital even if the other shareholders make proportionately smaller contributions, or no contribution at all. See, e.g., Sackstein v. Commissioner, 14 T.C. 566, 569 (1950). The rules governing contributions to capital reflect the general principle that a shareholder may not claim an immediate loss for outlays made to benefit the corporation. Deputy v. du Pont, 308 U.S. 488, 60 S.Ct. 363, 84 L.Ed. 416 (1940); Eskimo Pie Corp. v. Commissioner, 4 T.C. 669, 676 (1945), aff'd, 153 F.2d 301 (CA3 1946). We must decide whether this principle also applies to a controlling shareholder's non pro rata surrender of a portion of his shares.[6]

B

The Finks contend that they sustained an immediate loss upon surrendering some of their shares to the corporation. By parting with the shares, they gave up an ownership interest entitling them to future dividends, future capital appreciation, assets in the event of liquidation,

---

5. The Courts of Appeals for the Second and Fifth Circuits have held that a dominant shareholder's non pro rata stock surrender does not give rise to an ordinary loss. Frantz v. Commissioner, supra; Schleppy v. Commissioner, supra.

6. The Finks concede that a pro rata stock surrender, that by definition does not change the percentage ownership of any shareholder, is not a taxable event. Cf. Eisner v. Macomber, 252 U.S. 189, 40 S.Ct. 189, 64 L.Ed. 521 (1920) (pro rata stock dividend does not produce taxable income).

and voting rights.[7] Therefore, the Finks contend, they are entitled to an immediate deduction. See 26 U.S.C. §§ 165(a) and (c)(2). In addition, the Finks argue that any non pro rata stock transaction "give[s] rise to immediate tax results." Brief for Respondents 13. For example, a non pro rata stock divident produces income because it increases the recipient's proportionate ownership of the corporation. Koshland v. Helvering, 298 U.S. 441, 445, 56 S.Ct. 767, 769, 80 L.Ed. 1268 (1936).[8] By analogy, the Finks argue that a non pro rata surrender of shares should be recognized as an immediate loss because it reduces the surrendering shareholder's proportionate ownership.

Finally, the Finks contend that their stock surrenders were not contributions to the corporation's capital. They note that a typical contribution to capital, unlike a non pro rata stock surrender, has no effect on the contributing shareholder's proportionate interest in the corporation. Moreover, the Finks argue, a contribution of cash or other property increases the net worth of the corporation. For example, a shareholder's forgiveness of a debt owed to him by the corporation decreases the corporation's liabilities. In contrast, when a shareholder surrenders shares of the corporation's own stock, the corporation's net worth is unchanged. This is because the corporation cannot itself exercise the right to vote, receive dividends, or receive a share of assets in the event of liquidation. G. Johnson & J. Gentry, Finney and Miller's Principles of Accounting 538 (7th ed. 1974).[9]

III

A shareholder who surrenders a portion of his shares to the corporation has parted with an asset, but that alone does not entitle him to an immediate deduction. Indeed, if the shareholder owns less than 100 percent of the corporation's shares, any non pro rata contribution to the corporation's capital will reduce the net worth of the contributing shareholder.[10] A shareholder who surrenders stock thus is similar to

---

7. As a practical matter, however, the Finks did not give up a great deal. Their percentage interest in the corporation declined by only four percent. Because the Finks retained a majority interest, this reduction in their voting power was inconsequential. Moreover, Travco, like many corporations in financial difficulties, was not paying dividends.

8. In most cases, however, stock dividends are not recognized as income until the shares are sold. See 26 U.S.C. § 305.

9. Treasury stock—that is, stock that has been issued, reacquired by the corporation, and not canceled—generally is shown as an offset to shareholder's equity on the liability side of the balance sheet. G. Johnson & J. Gentry, Finney & Miller's Principles of Accounting 538 (7th ed. 1974).

10. For example, assume that a shareholder holding an 80 percent interest in a corporation with a total liquidation value of $100,000 makes a non pro rata contribution to the corporation's capital of $20,000 in cash. Assume further that the shareholder has no other assets. Prior to the contribution, the shareholder's net worth was $100,000 ($20,000 plus 80 percent of $100,000). If the corporation were immediately liquidated following the contribution, the shareholder would receive only $96,000 (80 percent of $120,000). Of course such a

Ch. 3 CAPITAL STRUCTURE OF A CORPORATION

one who forgives or surrenders a debt owed to him by the corporation; the latter gives up interest, principal, and also potential voting power in the event of insolvency or bankruptcy. But, as stated above, such forgiveness of corporate debt is treated as a contribution to capital rather than a current deduction. Supra, at 4. The Finks' voluntary surrender of shares, like a shareholder's voluntary forgiveness of debt owed by the corporation, closely resembles an investment or contribution to capital. See B. Bittker & J. Eustice, Federal Income Taxation of Corporations and Shareholders § 3.14, p. 3–59 (4th ed. 1979) ("If the contribution is voluntary, it does not produce gain or loss to the shareholder"). We find the similarity convincing in this case.

The fact that a stock surrender is not recorded as a contribution to capital on the corporation's balance sheet does not compel a different result. Shareholders who forgive a debt owed by the corporation or pay a corporate expense also are denied an immediate deduction, even though neither of these transactions is a contribution to capital in the accounting sense.[11] Nor are we persuaded by the fact that a stock surrender, unlike a typical contribution to capital, reduces the shareholder's proportionate interest in the corporation. This Court has never held that every change in a shareholder's percentage ownership has immediate tax consequences. Of course, a shareholder's receipt of property from the corporation generally is a taxable event. See 26 U.S.C. §§ 301, 316. In contrast, a shareholder's transfer of property to the corporation usually has no immediate tax consequences. § 263.

The Finks concede that the purpose of their stock surrender was to protect or increase the value of their investment in the corporation. Brief for Respondents 3.[12] They hoped to encourage new investors to provide needed capital and in the long run recover the value of the surrendered shares through increased dividends or appreciation in the value of their remaining shares. If the surrender had achieved its purpose, the Finks would not have suffered an economic loss. See Johnson, Tax Models for Nonprorata Shareholder Contributions, 3 Va.Tax.Rev. 81, 104–108 (1983). In this case, as in many cases involving closely-held corporations whose shares are not traded on an open market, there is no reliable method of determining whether the surrender will result in a loss until the shareholder disposes of his remaining shares. Thus, the Finks' stock surrender does not meet the require-

---

non pro rata contribution is rare in practice. Typically a shareholder will simply purchase additional shares.

11. It is true that a corporation's stock is not considered an asset of the corporation. A corporation's own shares nevertheless may be as valuable to the corporation as other property contributed by shareholders, as treasury shares may be resold.

This is evidenced by the fact that corporations often purchase their own shares on the open market.

12. Indeed, if the Finks did not make this concession their surrender probably would be treated as a non-deductible gift. See 26 CFR § 25.2511–1(h)(1) (1986).

ment that an immediately deductible loss must be "actually sustained during the taxable year." 26 CFR § 1.165–1(b) (1986).

Finally, treating stock surrenders as ordinary losses might encourage shareholders in failing corporations to convert potential capital losses to ordinary losses by voluntarily surrendering their shares before the corporation fails. In this way shareholders might avoid the consequences of 26 U.S.C. § 165(g)(1), that provides for capital loss treatment of stock that becomes worthless.[13] Similarly, shareholders may be encouraged to transfer corporate stock rather than other property to the corporation in order to realize a current loss.[14]

We therefore hold that a dominant shareholder who voluntarily surrenders a portion of his shares to the corporation, but retains control, does not sustain an immediate loss deductible from taxable income. Rather, the surrendering shareholder must reallocate his basis in the surrendered shares to the shares he retains.[15] The share-

13. The Tax Reform Act of 1986, Pub.L. 99–514, §§ 301, 311, 100 Stat. 2216, 2219 (Oct. 22, 1986), eliminated the differential tax rates for capital gains and ordinary income. The difference between a capital loss and an ordinary loss remains important, however, because individuals are permitted to deduct only $3,000 of capital losses against ordinary income each year, and corporations may not deduct any capital losses from ordinary income. 26 U.S.C. § 1211. In contrast, ordinary losses generally are deductible from ordinary income without limitation. §§ 165(a) and (c)(2).

The Court of Appeals in this case did not discuss the possibility of allowing a capital loss rather than an ordinary loss, and the parties raise it only in passing. We note, however that a capital loss is realized only upon the "sal[e] or exchang[e]" of a capital asset. 26 U.S.C. § 1211(b)(3). A voluntary surrender, for no consideration, would not seem to qualify as a sale or exchange. Frantz v. Commissioner, 784 F.2d, at 124.

14. Our holding today also draws support from two other sections of the Code. First, § 83 provides that, if a shareholder makes a "bargain sale" of stock to a corporate officer or employee as compensation, the "bargain" element of the sale must be treated as a contribution to the corporation's capital. S.Rep. No. 91–552, pp. 123–124 (1969), 1969 U.S.Code Cong. & Admin. News 1978, pp. 2027, 2155; 26 CFR § 1.83–6(d) (1986). Section 83 reversed the result in Downer v. Commissioner, 48 T.C. 86 (1967), a decision predicated on the fragmented view of stock ownership adopted by the Court of Appeals in this case. To be sure, Congress was concerned in § 83 with transfers of restricted stock to employees as compensation rather than surrenders of stock to improve the corporation's financial condition. In both cases, however, the shareholder's underlying purpose is to increase the value of his investment.

Second, if a shareholder's stock is redeemed—that is, surrendered to the corporation in return for cash or other property—the shareholder is not entitled to an immediate deduction unless the redemption results in a substantial reduction in the shareholder's ownership percentage. §§ 302(a), (b), (d); 26 CFR § 1.302–2(c) (1986). Because the Finks' surrenders resulted in only a slight reduction in their ownership percentage, they would not have been entitled to an immediate loss if they had received consideration for the surrendered shares. 26 U.S.C. § 302(b). Although the Finks did not receive a direct payment of cash or other property, they hoped to be compensated by an increase in the value of their remaining shares.

15. The Finks remained the controlling shareholders after their surrender. We therefore have no occasion to decide in this case whether a surrender that causes the shareholder to lose control of the corporation is immediately deductible. In related contexts, the Code distinguishes between minimal reductions in a shareholder's own-

holder's loss, if any, will be recognized when he disposes of his remaining shares. A reallocation of basis is consistent with the general principle that "[p]ayments made by a stockholder of a corporation for the purpose of protecting his interest therein must be regarded as [an] additional cost of his stock," and so cannot be deducted immediately. Eskimo Pie Corp. v. Commissioner, 4 T.C. 669, 676 (1945), aff'd, 153 F.2d 301 (CA3 1946). Our holding today is not inconsistent with the settled rule that the gain or loss on the sale or disposition of shares of stock equals the difference between the amount realized in the sale or disposition and the shareholder's basis in the particular shares sold or exchanged. See 26 U.S.C. § 1001(a); 26 CFR § 1.1012–1(c)(1) (1986). We conclude only that a controlling shareholder's voluntary surrender of shares, like contributions of other forms of property to the corporation, is not an appropriate occasion for the recognition of gain or loss.

In this case we use the term "control" to mean ownership of more than half of a corporation's voting shares. We recognize, of course, that in larger corporations—especially those whose shares are listed on a national exchange—a person or entity may exercise control in fact while owning less than a majority of the voting shares. See Securities Exchange Act of 1934, § 13(d), 48 Stat. 894, 15 U.S.C. § 78m(d) (requiring persons to report acquisition of more than 5 percent of a registered equity security).

IV

For the reasons we have stated, the judgment of the Court of Appeals for the Sixth Circuit is reversed.

It is so ordered.

Justice BLACKMUN concurs in the result.

Justice WHITE, concurring.

Although I join the Court's opinion, I suggest that there is little substance in the reservation in footnote 15 of the question whether a surrender of stock that causes the stockholder to lose control of the corporation is immediately deductible as an ordinary loss. Of course, this case does not involve a loss of control; but as I understand the rationale of the Court's opinion, it would also apply to a surrender that results in loss of control. At least I do not find in the opinion any principled ground for distinguishing a loss-of-control case from this one.

Justice SCALIA, concurring in the judgment.

ership percentage and loss of corporate control. See § 302(b)(2) (providing "exchange" rather than dividend treatment for a "substantially disproportionate redemption of stock" that brings the shareholder's ownership percentage below 50 percent); § 302(b)(3) (providing similar treatment when the redemption terminates the shareholder's interest in the corporation).

I do not believe that the Finks' surrender of their shares was, or even closely resembles, a shareholder contribution to corporate capital. Since, however, its purpose was to make the corporation a more valuable investment by giving it a more attractive capital structure, I think that it was, no less than a contribution to capital, an "amount paid out ... for ... betterments made to increase the value of ... property," 26 U.S.C. § 263(a)(1), and thus not entitled to treatment as a current deduction.

Justice STEVENS, dissenting.

The value of certain and predictable rules of law is often underestimated. Particularly in the field of taxation, there is a strong interest in enabling taxpayers to predict the legal consequences of their proposed actions, and there is an even stronger general interest in ensuring that the responsibility for making changes in settled law rests squarely on the shoulders of Congress. In this case, these interests are of decisive importance for me.

The question of tax law presented by this case was definitively answered by the Board of Tax Appeals in 1941. See Miller v. Commissioner, 45 B.T.A. 292, 299; Budd International Corp. v. Commissioner, 45 B.T.A. 737, 755–756.[1] Those decisions were consistently followed for over 40 years, see, e.g., Smith v. Commissioner, 66 T.C. 622, 648 (1976); Downer v. Commissioner, 48 T.C. 86, 91 (1967); Estate of Foster v. Commissioner, 9 T.C. 930, 934 (1947), and the Internal Revenue Service had announced its acquiescence in the decisions. See 1941–2 C.B. 9 (acquiescing in *Miller*); 1942–2 C.B. 3 (acquiescing in *Budd International*). Although Congress dramatically revamped the tax code in 1954, see Internal Revenue Code of 1954, Pub.L. 83–591, 68A Stat. 3, it did not modify the Tax Court's approach to this issue.

It was only in 1977 (after the Finks had transferred their stock to the corporation), that the Commission retracted its acquiescence in the Tax Court's interpretation.[2] But instead of asking Congress to reject the longstanding interpretation, the Commission asked the courts to take another look at the statute. Two Courts of Appeals accepted the Commission's new approach, and reversed the Tax Court without giving much, if any, weight to the Tax Court's nearly half-century old construction.[3] Tilford v. Commissioner, 705 F.2d 828 (CA6 1983); Schleppy

---

1. The principle applied in those decisions dates back even further. See Burdick v. Commissioner, 20 B.T.A. 742 (1930), aff'd, 59 F.2d 395 (1932); Wright v. Commissioner, 18 B.T.A. 471 (1929).

2. The Commission appears to have begun reconsidering its position around 1969. See Note, *Frantz or Fink*: Unitary or Fractional View for Non–Prorata Stock Surrenders, 48 U.Pitt.L.Rev. 905, 908–909 (1987) (hereafter Note).

3. Ignoring the import of the long line of Tax Court cases, one court stated: "We find no Court of Appeals decision that determines the correctness of these decisions. We therefore write on a clean sheet."

v. Commissioner, 601 F.2d 196 (CA5 1979). After these two reversals, the Tax Court itself reversed its position in 1984, believing that "[r]ecent appellate level disapproval of the position renders it inappropriate for us to continue to justify the position solely on the basis of its history." Frantz v. Commissioner, 83 T.C. 162, 174–182 (1984), aff'd, 784 F.2d 119 (CA2 1986), cert. pending, No. 86–11.

I believe that these courts erred in reversing the longstanding interpretation of the Tax Code. The Commissioner of Internal Revenue certainly had a right to advocate a change, but in my opinion he should have requested relief from the body that has the authority to amend the Internal Revenue Code. For I firmly believe that "after a statute has been construed, either by this Court or by a consistent course of decision by other federal judges and agencies, it acquires a meaning that should be as clear as if the judicial gloss had been drafted by the Congress itself." Shearson/American Express v. McMahon, 482 U.S. 220, ___, 107 S.Ct. 2332, 2359, 96 L.Ed.2d 185 (1987) (STEVENS, J., concurring in part and dissenting in part). A rule of statutory construction that "has been consistently recognized for more than 35 years" acquires a clarity that "is simply beyond peradventure." Herman & MacLean v. Huddleston, 459 U.S. 375, 380, 103 S.Ct. 683, 686, 74 L.Ed.2d 548 (1983).

There may, of course, be situations in which a past error is sufficiently blatant "to overcome the strong presumption of continued validity that adheres in the judicial interpretation of a statute." Square D Co. v. Niagara Frontier Tariff Bureau, 476 U.S. 409, 424, 106 S.Ct. 1922, 1930, 90 L.Ed.2d 413 (1986). But this is surely not such a case.[4] The Court makes no serious effort to demonstrate that its result is compelled by—or even consistent with—the language of the statute.[5]

Schleppy v. Commissioner, 601 F.2d 196, 198 (1979).

4. Strong arguments can be made in support of either view, as the split between the Second and Sixth Circuits, and the dissenting opinion of the four Tax Court Judges indicates. See Frantz v. Commissioner, 83 T.C. 162, 187 (1984) (Parker, J., with whom Fay, Goffe, and Wiles, JJ., joined, dissenting). See also Bolding, Non-Pro Rata Stock Surrenders: Capital Contribution, Capital Loss or Ordinary Loss?, 32 Tax Law. 275 (1979); Note, supra. Whether it makes sense to encourage stock surrenders that may enable a sinking corporation to stay afloat in cases like this is at least debatable. But whatever the correct policy choice may be, I would adhere to an interpretation of technical statutory language that has been followed consistently for over 40 years until Congress decides to change the law. Surely that is the wisest course when the language of the statute provides arguable support for the settled rule.

5. Uncharacteristically, the Court does not begin its analysis by quoting any statutory language, cf. Blue Chip Stamps v. Manor Drug Stores, 421 U.S. 723, 756, 95 S.Ct. 1917, 1935, 44 L.Ed.2d 539 (1975) (POWELL, J., concurring), either from § 165 of the Code, which defines "losses," or from § 1016, which deals with adjustments to basis. Rather, it launches into a discussion of voluntary contributions to capital, see ante, at 2732, even though this was clearly not such a contribution because it had no impact on the net worth of the corporation. The opinion includes a discussion of a hypothetical example, ante,

The mere fact that the Court's interpretation of the Internal Revenue Code may be preferable to the view that prevailed for years is not, in my opinion, a sufficient reason for changing the law.

If Congress lacked the power to amend statutes to rectify past mistakes, and if the only value to be achieved in construing statutes were accurate interpretation, it would be clear that a court or agency should feel free at any time to reject a past erroneous interpretation and replace it with the one it believes to be correct. But neither of these propositions is true; Congress does have the ability to rectify misinterpretations, and, once a statute has been consistently interpreted in one way, there are institutional and reliance values that are often even more important than the initial goal of accurate interpretation.

The relationship between the courts or agencies, on the one hand, and Congress, on the other, is a dynamic one. In the process of legislating it is inevitable that Congress will leave open spaces in the law that the courts are implicitly authorized to fill. The judicial process of construing statutes must therefore include an exercise of lawmaking power that has been delegated to the courts by the Congress. But after the gap has been filled, regardless of whether it is filled exactly as Congress might have intended or hoped, the purpose of the delegation has been achieved and the responsibility for making any future change should rest on the shoulders of the Congress. Even if it is a consensus of lower federal court decisions, rather than a decision by this Court, that has provided the answer to a question left open or ambiguous in the original text of the statute, there is really no need for this Court to revisit the issue. Moreover, if Congress understands that as long as a statute is interpreted in a consistent manner, it will not be re-examined by the courts except in the most extraordinary circumstances, Congress will be encouraged to give close scrutiny to judicial interpretations of its work product. We should structure our principles of statutory construction to invite continuing congressional oversight of the interpretive process.[6]

at 2733, n. 10, and policy reasons supporting the Court's result, but surprisingly little mention of statutory text. The statutory basis for the taxpayer's position is adequately explained in the opinions cited ante, at 2731, n. 3.

6. "The doctrine of *stare decisis* has a more limited application when the precedent rests on constitutional grounds, because 'correction through legislative action is practically impossible.' Burnet v. Coronado Oil & Gas Co., 285 U.S. 393, 407–408, 52 S.Ct. 443, 447–448, 76 L.Ed. 815 (Brandeis, J., dissenting). See Mitchell v. W.T. Grant Co., 416 U.S. 600, 627, 94 S.Ct. 1895, 1909, 40 L.Ed.2d 406 (POWELL, J., concurring)." Thomas v. Washington Gas Light Co., 448 U.S. 261, 272–273, n. 18, 100 S.Ct. 2647, 2656–2657, n. 18, 65 L.Ed.2d 757 (1980) (plurality opinion).

See also Edelman v. Jordan, 415 U.S. 651, 671, 94 S.Ct. 1347, 1359, 39 L.Ed.2d 662 (1974); Boys Markets v. Retail Clerks, 398 U.S. 235, 259–260, 90 S.Ct. 1583, 1596–1597, 26 L.Ed.2d 199 (1970) (Black, J., dissenting); Swift & Co. v. Wickham, 382 U.S. 111, 133–134, 86 S.Ct. 258, 270–271, 15 L.Ed.2d 194 (1965) (Douglas, J., dissenting).

Our readiness to reconsider long-settled constructions of statutes takes its toll on the courts as well. Except in the rarest of cases, I believe we should routinely follow Justice Cardozo's admonition:

"[T]he labor of judges would be increased almost to the breaking point if every past decision could be reopened in every case, and one could not lay one's own course of bricks on the secure foundation of the courses laid by others who had gone before him." B. Cardozo, The Nature of the Judicial Process 149 (1921).

In addition to the institutional ramifications of rejecting settled constructions of law, fairness requires consideration of the effect that changes have on individuals' reasonable reliance on a previous interpretation. This case dramatically illustrates the problem. Mr. Fink surrendered his shares in December 1976. Mrs. Fink surrendered hers in January 1977. At that time the law was well settled: the Tax Court had repeatedly reaffirmed the right to deduct such surrenders as ordinary losses, and the Commission had acquiesced in this view for 35 years.[7] See supra, p. 2736. It was only on April 11, 1977, that the Commission announced its nonacquiescence. See Internal Revenue Bulletin No. 1977-15, p. 6 (April 11, 1977). "In my view, the retroactive application of the Court's holding in a case like this is unfair to the individual taxpayer as well as unwise judicial administration." Dickman v. Commissioner, 465 U.S. 330, 353, n. 11, 104 S.Ct. 1086, 1094, n. 11, 79 L.Ed.2d 343 (1984) (POWELL, J., dissenting).

I respectfully dissent.

---

7. The Internal Revenue Service's Cumulative Bulletin explains the effect of an announcement of acquiescence:

"In order that taxpayers and the general public may be informed whether the Commissioner has acquiesced in a decision of the Tax Court of the United States, formally known as the United States Board of Tax Appeals, disallowing a deficiency in tax determined by the Commissioner to be due, announcement will be made in the semimonthly Internal Revenue Bulletin at the earliest practicable date. Notice that the Commissioner has acquiesced or nonacquiesced in a decision of the Tax Court relates only to the issue or issues decided adversely to the Government. *Decisions so acquiesced in should be relied upon by officers and employees of the Bureau of Internal Revenue as precedents in the disposition of other cases.*" 1942-2 C.B. IV (emphasis added).

CHAPTER 4. NONLIQUIDATING DISTRIBUTIONS

D. DISTRIBUTIONS OF PROPERTY

Page 148:

After the last full paragraph, add:

As discussed in the main volume, Section 301(b)(1)(B) had provided that the amount of a distribution to a corporate shareholder was the lesser of: (1) the fair market value of the property, or (2) its adjusted basis in the distributee's hands, increased by the amount of gain recognized by the distributing corporation on the distribution. Section 301(d)(2) generally provided that the corporate distributee's basis in the distributed property was the same as the amount of the distribution. Since the distributing corporation always recognizes gain on a nonliquidating distribution, these rules became a historical curiosity in that they required a comparison of two amounts which invariably were the same. (The rules made sense prior to repeal of the *General Utilities* doctrine.) Congress figured this out. The Technical and Miscellaneous Revenue Act of 1988 (hereafter referred to as "TAMRA") repealed most of former Section 301(b)(1) as deadwood and replaced it with a simple general rule providing that the amount of any Section 301 distribution is the amount of cash received plus the fair market value of any other property received. The basis rule in Section 301(d) was similarly simplified to remove any distinction between the basis of property received by corporate and noncorporate distributees.

F. ANTI-AVOIDANCE LIMITATIONS ON THE DIVIDENDS RECEIVED DEDUCTION

Page 160:

After the third full paragraph, insert:

TAMRA made several clarifying amendments to the extraordinary dividend rules in Section 1059, including:

> (1) The "dividend announcement date," with respect to which the two-year holding period requirement is tested, is now defined as the date on which the corporation declares, announces, or agrees to, the amount or payment of such dividend, whichever is the earliest. (§ 1059(d)(5)).

> (2) The "nontaxed portion" of any dividend that is either a non pro rata distribution or a partial liquidation distribution reduces

basis, without regard to whether the two-year holding period requirement is met. (§ 1059(e)(1)).

(3) The application of Section 1059(d)(6), which provides a special exception for dividends on stock held during the entire existence of the corporation, was clarified.

Page 162:

TAMRA redesignated Section 301(f) as Section 301(e); all references in the text should be changed accordingly.

Add to footnote 30:

In the 1987 Act, Congress amended Section 301(e) (formerly Section 301(f)) to provide that, in determining the character of a distribution to a 20 percent shareholder, earnings and profits are computed without regard to the depreciation adjustments in Section 312(k) or the other timing adjustments in Section 312(n). TAMRA then made it clear that the reference to Section 312(n) in Section 301(e) is to be treated as *not* including a reference to the rule in Section 312(n)(7) governing the effect of a redemption on earnings and profits.

Page 174:

In the Note, references to Section 301(f) should be changed to Section 301(e).

CHAPTER 5. REDEMPTIONS AND PARTIAL LIQUIDATIONS

C. REDEMPTIONS TESTED AT THE SHAREHOLDER LEVEL

Page 183:

After the last full paragraph, add:

In Revenue Ruling 87–88, 1987–2 C.B. 81, the Service considered how the substantially disproportionate safe harbor in Section 302(b)(2) should be applied when a corporation has more than one class of common stock outstanding and shares of each class are redeemed from one shareholder in one transaction. The Service ruled that Section 302(b)(2)(C), which provides that the fair market value of all of a corporation's common stock governs whether the requisite reduction in common stock ownership has occurred, suggests that the test should be applied on an aggregate rather than a class-by-class basis. Thus, if a shareholder's aggregate reduction in common stock (measured by value) meets the percentage tests in Section 302(b)(2)(C) (and the other requirements in Section 302(b)(2)), the redemption will be treated as an exchange even though the shareholder continues to own 100 percent of one class of outstanding common stock.

D. REDEMPTIONS TESTED AT THE CORPORATE LEVEL: PARTIAL LIQUIDATIONS

Page 220:

At the end of footnote 4, add:

For final regulations defining an active trade or business under Section 355, see Reg. § 1.355–3, discussed infra, this Supplement, pages 58–63.

E. CONSEQUENCES TO THE DISTRIBUTING CORPORATION

Page 229:

At the bottom of the page, insert:

In the 1987 Act, Congress enacted Section 5881, which imposes a 50 percent nondeductible excise tax on any gain realized from a "greenmail" payment. "Greenmail" is defined as any payment in redemption of stock held by a shareholder for less than two years where the shareholder has made or threatened an offer for the stock of that corporation within two years prior to the redemption. (§ 5881(b).) An

Ch. 5   *REDEMPTIONS AND PARTIAL LIQUIDATIONS*

exception is provided for redemptions made on the same terms from all shareholders. The tax applies to all greenmail payments made after December 22, 1987, with transitional exceptions. TAMRA clarified that the greenmail tax will be imposed on any gain or other income (e.g., including dividend income) of a person by reason of the receipt of greenmail.

G. REDEMPTIONS THROUGH RELATED CORPORATIONS

Page 259:

In the Code assignment, also omit § 304(b)(4).

Page 262:

After the first full paragraph, add:

As part of its effort to curtail techniques to avoid corporate-level tax on the disposition of unwanted assets following a corporate acquisition, Congress added Section 304(b)(4) in the 1987 Act. This amendment is discussed infra, this Supplement, page 30.

CHAPTER 7. COMPLETE LIQUIDATIONS AND TAXABLE DISPOSITIONS OF A CORPORATION'S ASSETS OR STOCK

B. COMPLETE LIQUIDATIONS

Page 312:

After the first full paragraph, add:

TAMRA clarified Section 453(h)(1)(B) to provide that the corporate "bulk sale" of inventory must be to one person in one transaction.

Page 316:

Add to footnote 18:

TAMRA amended Section 267(a)(1) to make it clear that its general loss disallowance rule does not apply either to any loss of the distributee or to any loss of the distributing corporation in the case of a distribution in complete liquidation. This clarification, however, does not preclude disallowance of losses under other provisions of the Code (e.g., Section 336(d)) or judicially created doctrines.

Page 319:

Add to footnote 30:

TAMRA amended Section 336(d)(2)(B)(ii) to make it clear that any property acquired in a Section 351 transaction or as a contribution to capital that was "acquired by the liquidated corporation after the date 2 years before the date of the adoption of the plan of complete liquidation" shall be treated (except as provided in regulations) as part of a "plan" to recognize loss by the corporation. This broader language would encompass built-in loss property acquired after the adoption of a liquidation plan.

Page 321:

After the first full paragraph, add:

In the General Explanation of the Tax Reform Act of 1986 and the Description of the Technical Corrections Act of 1988, the Joint Committee on Taxation elaborated on the operation of Section 336(d):

(1) In enacting Section 336(d), Congress did not intend to create any inference precluding the disallowance of losses in liquidating or nonliquidating distributions or sales under other statutory provisions (e.g., § 482) or judicial doctrines (e.g., assignment of income, business purpose or step transaction).

(2) If a transaction is described in both Sections 336(d)(1) and 336(d)(2), Section 336(d)(1) (which disallows the entire loss rather than just the precontribution built-in loss) will prevail.

(3) Congress intends the Treasury to issue regulations generally providing that the presumed prohibited tax avoidance purpose for contributions of property within two years of the adoption of a liquidation plan "will be disregarded unless there is no clear and substantial relationship between the contributed property and the conduct of the corporation's current or future business enterprises." In general, a "clear and substantial relationship" would generally include a requirement of a corporate business purpose for placing the property in the particular corporation to which it was contributed. If the contributed property has a built-in loss at the time of contribution that is "significant" relative to the built-in corporate gain at that time, "special scrutiny of the business purposes would be appropriate."

(4) Congress "expected" that the regulations will permit the allowance of any resulting loss from the disposition of any of the assets of a trade or business that are contributed to a corporation "where prior law would have permitted the allowance of the loss and the clear and substantial relationship test is satisfied." In those circumstances, Congress believed that application of Section 336(d) is inappropriate if there is a meaningful relationship between the contribution and the utilization of the particular corporate form to conduct a business enterprise. But if the contributed business is disposed of "immediately after" the contribution, the corporation will have difficulty showing that the "clear and substantial relationship" test was met.

(5) Congress "anticipated" that Section 336(d)(2) "will generally not apply" to a corporation's acquisition of property as part of its ordinary start-up or expansion of operations during its first two years of existence. But if a corporation has substantial gain assets during its first two years of operation, "a contribution of substantial built-in loss property followed by a sale or liquidation of the corporation would be expected to be closely scrutinized."

Staff of Joint Committee on Taxation, General Explanation of the Tax Reform Act of 1986, 100th Cong., 1st Sess. 341–346 (1987); Staff of Joint Committee on Taxation, Description of the Technical Corrections Act of 1988 (H.R. 4333 and S. 2238), 100th Cong., 2d Sess. 55–56 (1988). These interpretations are expected to be included in the regulations to be promulgated under Section 336(d).

For an excellent review of the post–1986 liquidations regime (and related issues) see Yin, "Taxing Corporate Liquidations (and Related Matters) After the Tax Reform Act of 1986," 42 Tax L. Rev. 573 (1987).

Page 324:

After the first full paragraph, add:

TAMRA amended Section 336(d)(3) to make it clear that the rule disallowing losses to a liquidating corporation on distributions to minority shareholders in a Section 332 liquidation applies only if the distribution does not result in gain recognition (e.g., on other distributed assets) to the distributing corporation under Sections 337(a) or (b)(1). If distributions in liquidation of a controlled subsidiary are not governed by the general Section 337 nonrecognition rules—e.g., because the controlling parent is a tax-exempt organization—the special loss disallowance rule in Section 336(d)(3) will not apply on any distributions to minority shareholders, but distributions of built-in loss property still are subject to any other applicable disallowance provisions (e.g., Sections 336(d)(1) or (d)(2)).

Page 325:

Add to footnote 7:

The technical correction predicted in the main volume has been made. TAMRA repealed former Section 334(b)(2); current Section 334(b)(2) (a corrected version of former Section 334(b)(3)) now defines "corporate distributee" for purposes of the basis rule in Section 334(b)(1).

In the second full paragraph, delete the third sentence, and insert:

Nonrecognition is restored, however, if the distributed property is used by the tax-exempt parent in an activity the income of which is subject to the unrelated business income tax under Section 511(a).

Page 326:

After the carryover paragraph, add:

If a corporation recognizes gain on a distribution in liquidation of a controlled subsidiary (e.g., on certain distributions to a tax-exempt or foreign corporation), Section 334(b)(1), as amended by TAMRA, makes it clear that the distributee takes a fair market value basis (rather than a transferred basis) in the distributed asset.

Ch. 7   *LIQUIDATION & SALES OF ASSETS OR STOCK*

Page 328:

The small corporation transitional rule expired at the end of 1988. Omit all the material from the first full paragraph on page 328 through the second full paragraph on page 330.

C. TAXABLE DISPOSITIONS OF A CORPORATE BUSINESS

Page 339:

The small corporation transitional rule expired at the end of 1988. Omit all the material from the first full paragraph on page 339 through the second full paragraph on page 340.

Page 341:

With the expiration of the small corporation transitional rule, parts (d), (e) and (g) of the Problem should be omitted.

Page 367:

After the carryover paragraph, add:

Reacting to contentions that the mirror subsidiary technique was incompatible with repeal of the *General Utilities* doctrine, Congress shattered the basic "mirror" strategy in the 1987 Act by adding the following new sentence to the definition of "80–percent distributee" in Section 337(c):

> For purposes of this section, the determination of whether any corporation is an 80–percent distributee shall be made without regard to any consolidated return regulation.

As indicated in the main volume, the aggregation of ownership rules in the consolidated return regulations (§ 1.1502–34) were essential to the success of the mirror subsidiary technique. After the 1987 amendment, however, a corporation will recognize gain on distributions in complete liquidation to a corporate shareholder unless the distributee directly owns 80 percent or more of the stock of the liquidating corporation. The Conference Report elaborated on the effect of this change:

> As under present law, gain will not be recognized by a corporation on liquidating distributions to a corporate shareholder directly owning 80 percent (by vote and value) of the stock of the distributing corporation. However, under the conference agreement, gain is recognized on any distribution to a corporation that does not meet the 80–percent test by direct ownership. Thus, for example, the distributing corporation recognizes gain on any distribution to a corporation within an affiliated group filing a consolidated tax return if the distributee would be treated as an 80–percent owner for purposes of section 332 solely by reason of the aggregation rules of section 1.1502–34 of the Treasury Regulations.

H.R.Rep. 100–495, 100th Cong., 1st Sess. 969 (1987). The Conference Report went on to authorize the Treasury to issue regulations providing that gain on a distribution to a less than 80 percent owner within an affiliated group of corporations filing a consolidated return may be deferred until a "recognition event" (e.g., a disposition of the asset outside of the group) other than the liquidation itself. Id. The amendment to Section 337 applies generally to distributions or transfers after December 15, 1987. 1987 Act § 10223(d).

The 1987 Act also curtailed more sophisticated variants of the mirror subsidiary technique by amendments to Section 304 (see new Section 304(b)(4), providing special treatment for certain transactions subject to Section 304(a) between members of an affiliated group of corporations) and to Section 355 (see amendments to Section 355(b)(2), discussed infra this Supplement at page 62.)

CHAPTER 9. PREVENTING THE IMPROPER RETENTION OF CORPORATE EARNINGS

B. THE ACCUMULATED EARNINGS TAX

Page 385:

Insert at footnote 3:

Correcting an obvious glitch, TAMRA changed the Section 531 accumulated earnings tax rate (formerly 27½ percent of the first $100,000 of accumulated taxable income and 38½ percent of the excess) to a flat 28 percent, effective for taxable years of the corporation beginning after December 31, 1987.

CHAPTER 10. ACQUISITIVE REORGANIZATIONS

B. TYPES OF ACQUISITIVE REORGANIZATIONS

Page 438:

After second full paragraph add:

NOTE

One of the more important recent cases to interpret and apply the step transaction doctrine is Esmark, Inc. v. Commissioner, 90 T.C. 171 (1988). Although *Esmark* involved a distribution of appreciated property in redemption prior to the 1986 Act amendments to Section 311, the case has broader significance insofar as the court held that the separate steps of a transaction structured by the parties to accomplish tax avoidance objectives would be respected rather than recast into a single integrated taxable transaction, as the Service had contended. An edited summary of the facts, followed by the court's discussion of the step transaction doctrine, is included below.

ESMARK, INC. v. COMMISSIONER
Tax Court of the United States, 1988.
90 T.C. 171.

COHEN, Judge:

[Edited Facts: The essential elements of the transaction in *Esmark* are not difficult to grasp. Esmark, Inc. was a diversified, publicly traded holding company. Among its wholly owned subsidiaries was Vickers, itself a holding company with several subsidiaries engaged in the oil business. Faced with liquidity problems and believing that the market price of its stock was undervalued, Esmark devised a restructuring plan. A major element of the plan was the sale of Vickers to the highest outside "bidder," which turned out to be Mobil Oil. Under the format chosen for the disposition, Esmark "invited" Mobil (which emerged as the high bidder after negotiations orchestrated by Esmark's investment bankers) to make a tender offer for approximately 54 percent of Esmark's stock—an amount roughly equivalent to the agreed value of the Vickers oil business. Mobil proceeded to make a tender and was successful in acquiring 54 percent of the stock. The next step, which was contemplated and agreed upon as part of the overall transaction, was the distribution by Esmark of its Vickers stock in redemption of the Esmark stock acquired by Mobil in the tender offer.

The parties conceded that the tender offer/redemption format was chosen in large part for the potential tax savings at the corporate level.

Although the Esmark shareholders who tendered their stock would recognize a capital gain (or loss) on the disposition of the shares (assuming they were not tax-exempt entities, such as pension funds), Esmark hoped to avoid any corporate-level gain on the appreciation inherent in the Vickers stock. Because the transaction occurred in 1980, prior to the piecemeal repeal of *General Utilities* discussed in Chapters 4, 5 and 7 of the text, Esmark relied on former Section 311(d)(2)(B), which then provided that a parent corporation would not recognize gain on a distribution of stock in a subsidiary (under specified conditions, all satisfied in *Esmark*) in redemption of the parent's stock.

The stakes were high. The Service claimed that Esmark owed over $150 million in taxes on a $452 million long-term capital gain on the distribution of the Vickers stock to Mobil. Relying on all the weapons it could find in the substance over form and step transaction arsenals, the Service recast the transaction as a sale by Esmark of its Vickers stock to Mobil followed by a redemption of the Esmark stock owned by the tendering shareholders for cash. The case involved the corporate-level tax consequences of the transaction.

Characterizing the case as "challenging," the Tax Court observed at the outset that "it must decide the primary issue under the rule and principles in effect at the time of the transaction despite historical criticism and subsequent abolition of that [*General Utilities*] rule" for "[t]o do otherwise would be to undermine as an essential ingredient of business decision-making (and as an art)." After rejecting a number of arguments advanced by the Service (a facts and circumstances analysis; assignment of income; Mobil was only a transitory owner and never a beneficial owner of the Esmark stock; and Mobil was a mere "conduit"), the court turned to the step transaction doctrine.]

The Step–Transaction Doctrine

Finally, respondent maintains that Mobil's ownership of the Esmark shares must be disregarded under the step-transaction doctrine. We recently described the step-transaction doctrine as another rule of substance over form that "treats a series of formally separate 'steps' as a single transaction if such steps are in substance integrated, interdependent, and focused toward a particular result." Penrod v. Commissioner, 88 T.C. 1415, 1428 (1987). Respondent contends that Mobil's acquisition and subsequent disposition of petitioner's shares were simply steps in an integrated transaction designed to result in Mobil's acquisition of Vickers and petitioner's redemption of its stock.

That Mobil's tender offer was but part of an overall plan is not in dispute. The existence of an overall plan does not alone, however, justify application of the step-transaction doctrine. Whether invoked as a result of the "binding commitment," "interdependence," or "end result" tests, the doctrine combines a series of individually meaningless steps into a single transaction. In this case, respondent has pointed to no meaningless or unnecessary steps that should be ignored.

Petitioner had two objectives: a disposition of its energy business and a redemption of a substantial portion of its stock. Three direct routes to these objectives were available:

First, petitioner could have distributed the Vickers stock to its shareholders in exchange for their shares. The shareholders could then have sold the Vickers stock for cash to interested buyers. See Commissioner v. Court Holding Co. and Cumberland Public Service Co. v. United States, supra.

Second, petitioner could have sold the Vickers stock for cash and then distributed the cash to its shareholders in exchange for their stock. As appears from our findings * * *, however, Mobil might not have been the successful bidder.

Third, the parties could have proceeded as they did, with Mobil purchasing petitioner's stock in a tender offer and exchanging such stock for the Vickers stock. No route was more "direct" than the others. Each route required two steps, and each step involved two of three interested parties. Each route left petitioner, petitioner's shareholders, and the purchaser in the same relative positions. Faced with this choice, petitioner chose the path expected to result in the least tax.

Respondent proposes to recharacterize the tender offer/redemption as a sale of the Vickers shares to Mobil followed by a self-tender. This recharacterization does not simply combine steps; it invents new ones. Courts have refused to apply the step-transaction doctrine in this manner. In Grove v. Commissioner, 490 F.2d 241 (2d Cir.1973), affg. a Memorandum Opinion of this Court, the Commissioner relied on the step-transaction doctrine to recharacterize a donor's gift of stock followed by a redemption of that stock from the donee as a redemption of the donor's shares followed by a gift of cash to the donee. The Court of Appeals stated:

> We are not so naive as to believe that tax considerations played no role in Grove's planning. But foresight and planning do not transform a non-taxable event into one that is taxable. Were we to adopt the Commissioner's view, we would be required to recast two actual transactions—a gift by Grove to RPI and a redemption from RPI by the Corporation—into two completely fictional transactions—a redemption from Grove by the Corporation and a gift by Grove to RPI. Based upon the facts as found by the Tax Court, we can discover no basis for elevating the Commissioner's "form" over that employed by the taxpayer in good faith. "Useful as the step transaction doctrine may be in the interpretation of equivocal contracts and ambiguous events, it cannot generate events which never took place just so

an additional tax liability might be asserted." Sheppard v. United States, [386 Ct.Cl. 982, 361 F.2d 972] supra, at 987 [(1966)]. [490 F.2d at 247–248.]

* * * On the basis of these precedents, we conclude that the step-transaction doctrine may not appropriately be applied in this case.

III. *Conclusion*

Although much more might be written about each of respondent's attacks on the form of petitioner's transaction, we have refrained from doing so. Stripped to its essentials, this case is a rematch of the principles expressed in Gregory v. Helvering, 293 U.S. 465 (1935), the source of most "substance over form" arguments.

In *Gregory,* the United Mortgage Co. (United) held among its assets 1,000 shares of the stock of Monitor Securities Corp. (Monitor). The taxpayer, United's sole shareholder, planned to sell the shares of Monitor and receive the proceeds of the sale. In order to avoid the double tax that would result if United sold the shares and distributed the proceeds as a dividend, the taxpayer had United contribute the stock of Monitor to a new corporation, which issued its stock to the taxpayer. This transaction was within the literal definition of "reorganization" under the law as then in effect. Following this "reorganization," the taxpayer dissolved the new corporation and sold the Monitor stock. The Supreme Court disregarded the form of the transaction as having no independent significance.

The Supreme Court framed the issue for decision as follows:

> The legal right of a taxpayer to decrease the amount of what otherwise would be his taxes, or altogether avoid them, by means which the law permits, cannot be doubted. But the question for determination is whether what was done, apart from the tax motive, was the thing which the statute intended. * * * [293 U.S. at 469. Citations omitted.]

In *Gregory,* the taxpayer's transaction was not "the thing that the statute intended" because a reorganization, as that term was defined in the statute, did not in fact take place:

> Putting aside, then, the question of motive in respect of taxation altogether, and fixing the character of the proceeding by what actually occurred, what do we find? Simply an operation having no business or corporate purpose —a mere device which put on the form of a corporate reorganization as a disguise for concealing its real character, and the sole object and accomplishment of which was the consummation of a preconceived plan, not to reorganize a business or any part of a business, but to transfer a parcel of corporate shares to the petitioner. No doubt, a new and valid corporation was created. But that corporation was nothing more than a contrivance to the end last described. It was brought into existence for no other purpose; it performed, as it was intended from the beginning it should perform, no

other function. When that limited function had been exercised, it immediately was put to death. [293 U.S. at 469–470.]

In this case, in contrast, there were no steps without independent function. Each of the steps—the purchase of petitioner's stock by Mobil and the redemption of that stock by petitioner—had permanent economic consequences. Mobil's tender offer was not a "mere device" having no business purpose; the tender offer was an essential element of petitioner's plan to redeem over 50 percent of its stock. Mobil's ownership, however transitory, must thus be respected, and if Mobil's ownership of petitioner's shares is respected, a "distribution with respect to * * * stock" in fact occurred.

But was this transaction truly the "thing that the statute intended?" As discussed above, section 311(a) is said to be the codification of the *General Utilities* doctrine. The rationale behind that doctrine has never been clearly articulated. Presumably, the doctrine represents an attempt to ameliorate the perceived harshness of the two-tier system of corporate taxation. Lewis, "A Proposed New Treatment For Corporate Distributions and Sales in Liquidation," Tax Review Compendium 1643, Staff of House Comm. on Ways and Means, 86th Cong., 1st Sess. (Comm.Print 1959). The doctrine may also rest on the belief that a corporation receives nothing of value for its assets when it makes a dividend distribution or redeems its stock with property. In Houston Bros. Co. v. Commissioner, 21 B.T.A. 804 (1930), the Board of Tax Appeals explained the principle as follows:

> It is quite possible that, by disposing of some of its assets in exchange for or retirement of some of its outstanding shares, a corporation may be in a stronger financial position than before. But this means only that the distributive interests of its shareholders have been potentially improved. The assets of the corporation itself are not more or of greater value. They are actually less, and only the proportionate value of the shares still in the hands of shareholders has been increased. Before it can be said that the corporation has profit, it must be found not only that it has disposed of its property, but that it has received assets of greater value than the cost of those disposed of. But since a corporation's own shares are not assets, but only the convenient machinery for evidencing shareholder interests, it is a fallacy to say it has received anything and *a fortiori* that it has received a gain. * * * [21 B.T.A. at 815.]

In United States v. General Geophysical Co., 296 F.2d 86 (5th Cir.1961), the Court of Appeals for the Fifth Circuit used similar reasoning to explain section 311(a):

> The rule may be easily justified by the fact that when a corporation transfers appreciated property to its shareholders, as a dividend or in exchange for their shares, the gain created by the appreciation has not accrued to the corporation and should not be taxed to it. [296 F.2d at 88. Fn. ref. omitted.]

The focus of section 311(a) is on the position of the corporation before and after the transaction rather than on the identity of the shareholder who surrendered stock. Given this explanation of the "policy" behind the *General Utilities* doctrine, we cannot say that petitioner's transaction was not "the thing that the statute intended."

In an economic sense, there is no difference between the form chosen by petitioner and the "substance" alleged by respondent. In this instance, however, tax treatment is dictated by form. That this situation is far from unusual is illustrated by the Supreme Court's decisions in *Court Holding* and *Cumberland Public Service.* As the Court noted in the latter case:

> The oddities in tax consequences that emerge from the tax provisions here controlling appear to be inherent in the present tax pattern. For a corporation is taxed if it sells all its physical properties and distributes the cash proceeds as liquidating dividends, yet is not taxed if that property is distributed in kind and is then sold by the shareholders. In both instances the interest of the shareholders in the business has been transferred to the purchaser. * * *
>
> Congress having determined that different tax consequences shall flow from different methods by which the shareholders of a closely held corporation may dispose of corporate property, we accept its mandate. * * *
>
> [338 U.S. at 455–456.]

We, too, must accept the mandate of Congress, particularly where the corporation is publicly and not closely held. Congress resolved the *Court Holding* issue by enacting section 337. For future years, Congress has resolved the issue presented in this case by abolishing the *General Utilities* doctrine altogether. Tax Reform Act of 1986, Pub.L. 99–514, 100 Stat. 2085. In 1980, however, petitioner was entitled to rely on the literal language of section 311, and the judicially recognized doctrines give us no satisfactory basis for taxing the transaction as if something else had occurred. See Grove v. Commissioner, supra. We have carefully considered the arguments of the parties set forth in their excellent briefs. We believe that ad hoc extension of doctrine to achieve a result on any of the difficult issues in this case is unwarranted and unwise.

Page 478:

After the second full paragraph, insert:

REVENUE RULING 88–48
1988–1 Cum.Bull. 117.

ISSUE

If a transferor corporation sold 50 percent of its historic assets to unrelated parties for cash and immediately afterwards transferred to an acquiring corporation all of its assets (including the cash from the sale), did the subsequent transfer meet the "substantially all" requirement of section 368(a)(1)(C) of the Internal Revenue Code?

FACTS

X and Y were unrelated corporations that for many years were engaged in the hardware business. X operated two significant lines of business, a retail hardware business and a wholesale plumbing supply business. Y desired to acquire and continue to operate X's hardware business but did not desire to acquire the other business. Accordingly, pursuant to an overall plan, the following steps were taken. First, in a taxable transaction, X sold its entire interest in the plumbing supply business (constituting 50 percent of its total historic business assets) to purchasers unrelated to either X or Y or their shareholders. Second, X transferred all of its assets, including the cash proceeds from the sale, to Y solely for Y voting stock and the assumption of X's liabilities. Finally, in pursuance of the plan of reorganization, X distributed the Y stock (the sole asset X then held) to the X shareholders in complete liquidation.

Except for the issue relating to the "substantially all" requirement, the transfer of assets from X to Y constituted a corporate reorganization within the meaning of section 368(a)(1)(C) of the Code.

LAW AND ANALYSIS

Section 368(a)(1)(C) of the Code defines a corporate reorganization to include the acquisition by one corporation, in exchange solely for all or part of its voting stock, of substantially all the properties of another corporation.

Section 368(a)(1)(C) of the Code is intended to accommodate transactions that are, in effect, mergers, but which fail to meet the statutory requirements that would bring them within section 368(a)(1)(A). See S.Rep. No. 558, 73d Cong., 2d Sess. 16, 17 (1939), 1939–1 C.B. (Pt. 2) 586, 598.

Congress intended that transactions that are divisive in nature not qualify under section 368(a)(1)(C) of the Code, but, instead, be subject to the tests under section 368(a)(1)(D). See S.Rep. No. 1622, 83d Cong., 2d Sess. 274 (1954). The enactment of section 368(a)(2)(G) indicates the continuing interest in furthering this underlying objective of preventing divisive "C" reorganizations.

Rev.Rul. 57–518, 1957–2 C.B. 253, concerns whether, in a "C" reorganization, assets may be retained to pay liabilities. The ruling states that what constitutes "substantially all" for purposes of section 368(a)(1)(C) of the Code depends on the facts and circumstances in each case. Rev.Rul. 57–518 exemplifies the Service's longstanding position that where some assets are transferred to the acquiring corporation and other assets retained, then the transaction may be divisive and so fail to meet the "substantially all" requirement of section 368(a)(1)(C). See also Rev.Rul. 78–47, 1978–1 C.B. 113.

In the present situation, 50 percent of the X assets acquired by Y consisted of cash from the sale of one of X's significant historic businesses. Although Y acquired substantially all the assets X held at the time of transfer, the prior sale prevented Y from acquiring substantially all of X's historic business assets. The transaction here at issue, however, was not divisive. The sale proceeds were not retained by the transferor corporation or its shareholders, but were transferred to the acquiring corporation. Moreover, the prior sale of the historic business assets was to unrelated purchasers, and the X shareholders retained no interest, direct or indirect, in these assets. Under these circumstances, the "substantially all" requirement of section 368(a)(1)(C) was met because all of the assets of X were transferred to Y.

HOLDING

The transfer of all of its assets by X to Y met the "substantially all" requirement of section 368(a)(1)(C) of the Code, even though immediately prior to the transfer X sold 50 percent of its historic business assets to unrelated parties for cash and transferred that cash to Y instead of the historic assets.

C. TREATMENT OF THE PARTIES TO AN ACQUISITIVE REORGANIZATION

Page 488:

Delete the Tax Court opinion in Clark, and insert:

COMMISSIONER v. CLARK *

Supreme Court of the United States, 1989.
___ U.S. ___, 109 S.Ct. 1455.

Justice STEVENS delivered the opinion of the Court. This is the third case in which the Government has asked us to decide that a shareholder's receipt of a cash payment in exchange for a portion of his stock was taxable as a dividend. In the two earlier cases, Commissioner v. Estate of Bedford, 325 U.S. 283 (1945), and United States v. Davis, 397 U.S. 301 (1970), we agreed with the Government largely because the transactions involved redemptions of stock by single corporations that did not "result in a meaningful reduction of the shareholder's proportionate interest in the corporation." Id., at 313. In the case we decide today, however, the taxpayer in an arm's length transaction

---

* Some footnotes omitted.

exchanged his interest in the acquired corporation for less than one percent of the stock of the acquiring corporation and a substantial cash payment. The taxpayer held no interest in the acquiring corporation prior to the reorganization. Viewing the exchange as a whole, we conclude that the cash payment is not appropriately characterized as a dividend. We accordingly agree with the Tax Court and with the Court of Appeals that the taxpayer is entitled to capital gains treatment of the cash payment.

I

In determining tax liability under the Internal Revenue Code, gain resulting from the sale or exchange of property is generally treated as capital gain, whereas the receipt of cash dividends is treated as ordinary income.[2] The Code, however, imposes no current tax on certain stock-for-stock exchanges. In particular, § 354(a)(1) provides, subject to various limitations, for nonrecognition of gain resulting from the exchange of stock or securities solely for other stock or securities, provided that the exchange is pursuant to a plan of corporate reorganization and that the stock or securities are those of a party to the reorganization. 26 U.S.C. § 354(a)(1).

Under § 356(a)(1) of the Code, if such a stock-for-stock exchange is accompanied by additional consideration in the form of a cash payment or other property—something that tax practitioners refer to as "boot"— "then the gain, if any, to the recipient shall be recognized, but in an amount not in excess of the sum of such money and the fair market value of such other property." 26 U.S.C. § 356(a)(1). That is, if the shareholder receives boot, he or she must recognize the gain on the exchange up to the value of the boot. Boot is accordingly generally treated as a gain from the sale or exchange of property and is recognized in the current tax-year.

Section 356(a)(2), which controls the decision in this case, creates an exception to that general rule. It provides:

"If an exchange is described in paragraph (1) but has the effect of the distribution of a dividend (determined with the application of section 318(a)), then there shall be treated as a dividend to each distributee such an amount of the gain recognized under paragraph

2. In 1979, the tax year in question, the distinction between long-term capital gain and ordinary income was of considerable importance. Most significantly, § 1202(a) of the Code allowed individual taxpayers to deduct 60% of their net capital gain from gross income. Although the importance of the distinction declined dramatically in 1986 with the repeal of § 1202(a), see Tax Reform Act of 1986, Pub.L. 99–514, § 301(a), 100 Stat. 2216, the distinction is still significant in a number of respects. For example, § 1211(b) allows individual taxpayers to deduct capital losses to the full extent of their capital gains, but only allows them to offset up to $3000 of ordinary income insofar as their capital losses exceed their capital gains.

Ch. 10   *ACQUISITIVE REORGANIZATIONS*

(1) as is not in excess of his ratable share of the undistributed earnings and profits of the corporation accumulated after February 28, 1913. The remainder, if any, of the gain recognized under paragraph (1) shall be treated as gain from the exchange of property."

Thus, if the "exchange ... has the effect of the distribution of a dividend," the boot must be treated as a dividend and is therefore appropriately taxed as ordinary income to the extent that gain is realized. In contrast, if the exchange does not have "the effect of the distribution of a dividend," the boot must be treated as a payment in exchange for property and, insofar as gain is realized, accorded capital gains treatment. The question in this case is thus whether the exchange between the taxpayer and the acquiring corporation had "the effect of the distribution of a dividend" within the meaning of § 356(a)(2).

The relevant facts are easily summarized. For approximately 15 years prior to April 1979, the taxpayer was the sole shareholder and president of Basin Surveys, Inc. (Basin), a company in which he had invested approximately $85,000. The corporation operated a successful business providing various technical services to the petroleum industry. In 1978, N.L. Industries, Inc. (NL), a publicly owned corporation engaged in the manufacture and supply of petroleum equipment and services, initiated negotiations with the taxpayer regarding the possible acquisition of Basin. On April 3, 1979, after months of negotiations, the taxpayer and NL entered into a contract.

The agreement provided for a "triangular merger," whereby Basin was merged into a wholly owned subsidiary of NL. In exchange for transferring all of the outstanding shares in Basin to NL's subsidiary, the taxpayer elected to receive 300,000 shares of NL common stock and cash boot of $3,250,000, passing up an alternative offer of 425,000 shares of NL common stock. The 300,000 shares of NL issued to the taxpayer amounted to approximately 0.92% of the outstanding common shares of NL. If the taxpayer had instead accepted the pure stock-for-stock offer, he would have held approximately 1.3% of the outstanding common shares. The Commissioner and the taxpayer agree that the merger at issue qualifies as a reorganization under § 368(a)(1)(A) and (a)(2)(D).

Respondents filed a joint federal income tax return for 1979. As required by § 356(a)(1), they reported the cash boot as taxable gain. In calculating the tax owed, respondents characterized the payment as long-term capital gain. The Commissioner on audit disagreed with this characterization. In his view, the payment had "the effect of the distribution of a dividend" and was thus taxable as ordinary income up to $2,319,611, the amount of Basin's accumulated earnings and profits at the time of the merger. The Commissioner assessed a deficiency of $972,504.74.

Respondents petitioned for review in the Tax Court, which, in a reviewed decision, held in their favor. 86 T.C. 138 (1986). The court started from the premise that the question whether the boot payment had "the effect of the distribution of a dividend" turns on the choice between "two judicially articulated tests." Id., at 140. Under the test advocated by the Commissioner and given voice in Shimberg v. United States, 577 F.2d 283 (CA–5 1978), cert. denied, 439 U.S. 1115 (1979), the boot payment is treated as though it were made in a hypothetical redemption by the acquired corporation (Basin) immediately *prior* to the reorganization. Under this test, the cash payment received by the taxpayer indisputably would have been treated as a dividend.[6] The second test, urged by the taxpayer and finding support in Wright v. United States, 482 F.2d 600 (CA–8 1973), proposes an alternative hypothetical redemption. Rather than concentrating on the taxpayer's pre-reorganization interest in the acquired corporation, this test requires that one imagine a pure stock-for-stock exchange, followed immediately by a *post*-reorganization redemption of a portion of the taxpayer's shares in the acquiring corporation (NL) in return for a payment in an amount equal to the boot. Under § 302 of the Code, which defines when a redemption of stock should be treated as a distribution of dividend, NL's redemption of 125,000 shares of its stock from the taxpayer in exchange for the $3,250,000 boot payment would have been treated as capital gain.[7]

---

6. The parties do not agree as to whether dividend equivalence for the purposes of § 356(a)(2) should be determined with reference to § 302 of the Code, which concerns dividend treatment of redemptions of stock by a single corporation outside the context of a reorganization. Compare Brief for the United States 28–30 with Brief for Respondents 18–24. They are in essential agreement, however, about the characteristics of a dividend. Thus, the Government correctly argues that the "basic attribute of a dividend, derived from Sections 301 and 316 of the Code, is a pro rata distribution to shareholders out of corporate earnings and profits. When a distribution is made that is not a formal dividend, 'the fundamental test of dividend equivalency' is whether the distribution is proportionate to the shareholders' stock interests (United States v. Davis, 397 U.S. 301, 306 (1970))." Brief for Petitioner 7. Citing the same authority, but with different emphasis, the taxpayer argues that "the hallmark of a non-dividend distribution is a 'meaningful reduction of the shareholder's proportionate interest in the corporation,' United States v. Davis, 397 U.S. 301, 313 (1970)." Brief for Respondents 5.

Under either test, a pre-reorganization distribution by Basin to the taxpayer would have qualified as a dividend. Because the taxpayer was Basin's sole shareholder, any distribution necessarily would have been pro rata and would not have resulted in a "meaningful reduction of the [taxpayer's] proportionate interest in [Basin]."

7. * * *

As the Tax Court explained, receipt of the cash boot reduced the taxpayer's potential holdings in NL from 1.3% to 0.92%. 86 T.C., at 153. The taxpayer's holdings were thus approximately 71% of what they would have been absent the payment. Ibid. This fact, combined with the fact that the taxpayer held less than 50% of

Ch. 10   ACQUISITIVE REORGANIZATIONS

The Tax Court rejected the pre-reorganization test favored by the Commissioner because it considered it improper "to view the cash payment as an isolated event totally separate from the reorganization." 86 T.C., at 151. Indeed, it suggested that this test requires that courts make the "determination of dividend equivalency fantasizing that the reorganization does not exist." Id., at 150 (footnote omitted). The court then acknowledged that a similar criticism could be made of the taxpayer's contention that the cash payment should be viewed as a post-reorganization redemption. It concluded, however, that since it was perfectly clear that the cash payment would not have taken place without the reorganization, it was better to treat the boot "as the equivalent of a redemption *in the course of implementing the reorganization*," than "as having occurred *prior to and separate from the reorganization*." Id., at 152 (emphasis in original).[8]

The Court of Appeals for the Fourth Circuit affirmed. 828 F.2d 221 (1987). Like the Tax Court, it concluded that although "[s]ection 302 does not explicitly apply in the reorganization context," id., at 223, and although § 302 differs from § 356 in important respects, id., at 224, it nonetheless provides "the appropriate test for determining whether boot is ordinary income or a capital gain," id., at 223. Thus, as explicated in § 302(b)(2), if the taxpayer relinquished more than 20% of his corporate control and retained less than 50% of the voting shares after the distribution, the boot would be treated as capital gain. However, as the Court of Appeals recognized, "[b]ecause § 302 was designed to deal with a stock redemption by a single corporation, rather than a

---

the voting stock of NL after the hypothetical redemption, would have qualified the "distribution" as "substantially disproportionate" under § 302(b)(2).

8. The Tax Court stressed that to adopt the pre-reorganization view "would in effect resurrect the now discredited 'automatic dividend rule' ..., at least with respect to pro rata distributions made to an acquired corporation's shareholders pursuant to a plan of reorganization." 86 T.C., at 152. On appeal, the Court of Appeals agreed. [87–2 USTC ¶ 9504] 828 F.2d 221, 226–227 (CA–4 1987).

The "automatic dividend rule" developed as a result of some imprecise language in our decision in Commissioner v. Estate of Bedford, 325 U.S. 283 (1945). Although *Estate of Bedford* involved the recapitalization of a single corporation, the opinion employed broad language, asserting that "a distribution, pursuant to a reorganization, of earnings and profits 'has the effect of a distribution of a taxable dividend' within [§ 356(a)(2)]." Id., at 292. The Commissioner read this language as establishing as a matter of law that all payments of boot are to be treated as dividends to the extent of undistributed earnings and profits. See Rev.Rul. 56–220, 1956–1 Cum.Bull. 191. Commentators, see, e.g., Darrel, The Scope of Commissioner v. Bedford Estate, 24 TAXES 266 (1946); Shoulson, Boot Taxation: The Blunt Toe of the Automatic Rule, 20 Tax L.Rev. 573 (1965), and courts, see, e.g., Hawkinson v. Commissioner, 235 F.2d 747 (CA–2 1966), however, soon came to criticize this rule. The courts have long since retreated from the "automatic dividend rule," see, e.g., Idaho Power Co. v. United States, 161 F.Supp. 807 (Ct.Cl.), cert. denied, 368 U.S. 832 (1968), and the Commissioner has followed suit, see Rev.Rul. 74–515, 1974–2 Cum.Bull. 118. As our decision in this case makes plain, we agree that *Estate of Bedford* should not be read to require that all payments of boot be treated as dividends.

reorganization involving two companies, the section does not indicate which corporation [the taxpayer] lost interest in." Id., at 224. Thus, like the Tax Court, the Court of Appeals was left to consider whether the hypothetical redemption should be treated as a pre-reorganization distribution coming from the acquired corporation or as a post-reorganization distribution coming from the acquiring corporation. It concluded:

> "Based on the language and legislative history of § 356, the change-in-ownership principle of § 302, and the need to review the reorganization as an integrated transaction, we conclude that the boot should be characterized as a post-reorganization stock redemption by N.L. that affected [the taxpayer's] interest in the new corporation. Because this redemption reduced [the taxpayer's] N.L. holdings by more than 20%, the boot should be taxed as a capital gain." Id., at 224–225.

This decision by the Court of Appeals for the Fourth Circuit is in conflict with the decision of the Fifth Circuit in *Shimberg,* 577 F.2d 283 (1978), in two important respects. In *Shimberg,* the court concluded that it was inappropriate to apply stock redemption principles in reorganization cases "on a wholesale basis." Id., at 287; see also ibid, n. 13. In addition, the court adopted the pre-reorganization test, holding that "§ 356(a)(2) requires a determination of whether the distribution would have been taxed as a dividend if made prior to the reorganization or if no reorganization had occurred." Id., at 288.

To resolve this conflict on a question of importance to the administration of the federal tax laws, we granted certiorari. 485 U.S. ___ (1988).

II

We agree with the Tax Court and the Court of Appeals for the Fourth Circuit that the question under § 356(a)(2) of whether an "exchange ... has the effect of the distribution of a dividend" should be answered by examining the effect of the exchange as a whole. We think the language and history of the statute, as well as a common-sense understanding of the economic substance of the transaction at issue, support this approach.

The language of § 356(a) strongly supports our understanding that the transaction should be treated as an integrated whole. Section 356(a)(2) asks whether "*an exchange* is described in paragraph (1)" that "has the effect of the distribution of a dividend." (Emphasis supplied.) The statute does not provide that boot shall be treated as a dividend if its payment has the effect of the distribution of a dividend. Rather, the inquiry turns on whether the "exchange" has that effect. Moreover, paragraph (1), in turn, looks to whether "the property received in *the exchange* consists not only of property permitted by section 354 or 355 to be received without the recognition of gain but also of other property or money." (Emphasis supplied.) Again, the statute plainly refers to one integrated transaction and, again, makes clear that we are to look to the character of the exchange as a whole and not simply its component parts. Finally, it is significant that § 356 expressly limits the extent to which boot may be taxed to the amount of gain realized in the reorganization. This limitation suggests that Congress intended that boot not be treated in isolation from the overall reorganization. See Levin, Adess, & McGaffey, Boot Distributions in Corporate Reorganizations—Determination of Dividend Equivalency, 30 Tax Lawyer 287, 303 (1977).

Our reading of the statute as requiring that the transaction be treated as a unified whole is reinforced by the well-established "step-transaction" doctrine, a doctrine that the Government has applied in related contexts, see, e.g., Rev.Rul. 75–447, 1975–2 Cum.Bull. 113, and that we have expressly sanctioned, see Minnesota Tea Co. v. Helvering, 302 U.S. 609, 613 (1938); Commissioner v. Court Holding Co., 324 U.S. 331, 334 (1945). Under this doctrine, interrelated yet formally distinct steps in an integrated transaction may not be considered independently of the overall transaction. By thus "linking together all interdependent steps with legal or business significance, rather than taking them in isolation," federal tax liability may be based "on a realistic view of the entire transaction." 1 B. Bittker, Federal Taxation of Income, Estates and Gifts, ¶ 4.3.5, p. 4–52 (1981).

Viewing the exchange in this case as an integrated whole, we are unable to accept the Commissioner's pre-reorganization analogy. The analogy severs the payment of boot from the context of the reorganization. Indeed, only by straining to abstract the payment of boot from the context of the overall exchange, and thus imagining that Basin made a distribution to the taxpayer independently of NL's planned acquisition, can we reach the rather counterintuitive conclusion urged by the Commissioner—that the taxpayer suffered no meaningful reduction in his ownership interest as a result of the cash payment. We conclude that such a limited view of the transaction is plainly inconsistent with the statute's direction that we look to the effect of the entire exchange.

The pre-reorganization analogy is further flawed in that it adopts an overly expansive reading of § 356(a)(2). As the Court of Appeals recognized, adoption of the pre-reorganization approach would "result in ordinary income treatment in most reorganizations because corporate boot is usually distributed pro rata to the shareholders of the target corporation." 828 F.2d, at 227; see also Golub, "Boot" in

Reorganizations—The Dividend Equivalency Test of Section 356(a)(2), 58 Taxes 904, 911 (1980); Note, 20 Boston College L.Rev. 601, 612 (1979). Such a reading of the statute would not simply constitute a return to the widely criticized "automatic dividend rule" (at least as to cases involving a pro rata payment to the shareholders of the acquired corporation), see n. 8, supra, but also would be contrary to our standard approach to construing such provisions. The requirement of § 356(a)(2) that boot be treated as dividend in some circumstances is an exception from the general rule authorizing capital gains treatment for boot. In construing provisions such as § 356, in which a general statement of policy is qualified by an exception, we usually read the exception narrowly in order to preserve the primary operation of the provision. See Phillips, Inc. v. Walling, 324 U.S. 490, 493 (1945) ("To extend an exemption to other than those plainly and unmistakably within its terms and spirit is to abuse the interpretative process and to frustrate the announced will of the people"). Given that Congress has enacted a general rule that treats boot as capital gain, we should not eviscerate that legislative judgment through an expansive reading of a somewhat ambiguous exception.

The post-reorganization approach adopted by the Tax Court and the Court of Appeals is, in our view, preferable to the Commissioner's approach. Most significantly, this approach does a far better job of treating the payment of boot as a component of the overall exchange. Unlike the pre-reorganization view, this approach acknowledges that there would have been no cash payment absent the exchange and also that, by accepting the cash payment, the taxpayer experienced a meaningful reduction in his potential ownership interest.

Once the post-reorganization approach is adopted, the result in this case is pellucidly clear. Section 302(a) of the Code provides that if a redemption fits within any one of the four categories set out in § 302(b), the redemption "shall be treated as a distribution in part or full payment in exchange for the stock," and thus not regarded as a dividend. As the Tax Court and the Court of Appeals correctly determined, the hypothetical post-reorganization redemption by NL of a portion of the taxpayer's shares satisfies at least one of the subsections of § 302(b).[9] In particular, the safe harbor provisions of subsection (b)(2) provide that redemptions in which the taxpayer relinquishes more than 20% of his or her share of the corporation's voting stock and retains less than 50% of the voting stock after the redemption, shall

---

9. Because the mechanical requirements of subsection (b)(2) are met, we need not decide whether the hypothetical redemption might also qualify for capital gains treatment under the general "not essentially equivalent to a dividend" language of subsection (b)(1). Subsections (b)(3) and (b)(4), which deal with redemptions of all of the shareholder's stock and with partial liquidations, respectively, are not at issue in this case.

not be treated as distributions of a dividend. See n. 7, supra. Here, we treat the transaction as though NL redeemed 125,000 shares of its common stock (i.e., the number of shares of NL common stock foregone in favor of the boot) in return for a cash payment to the taxpayer of $3,250,000 (i.e., the amount of the boot). As a result of this redemption, the taxpayer's interest in NL was reduced from 1.3% of the outstanding common stock to 0.9%. See 86 T.C., at 153. Thus, the taxpayer relinquished approximately 29% of his interest in NL and retained less than a 1% voting interest in the corporation after the transaction, easily satisfying the "substantially disproportionate" standards of § 302(b)(2). We accordingly conclude that the boot payment did not have the effect of a dividend and that the payment was properly treated as capital gain.

III

The Commissioner objects to this "recasting [of] the merger transaction into a form different from that entered into by the parties," Brief for the United States 11, and argues that the Court of Appeals' formal adherence to the principles embodied in § 302 forced the court to stretch to "find a redemption to which to apply them, since the merger transaction entered into by the parties did not involve a redemption," id., at 28. There are a number of sufficient responses to this argument. We think it first worth emphasizing that the Commissioner overstates the extent to which the redemption is imagined. As the Court of Appeals for the Fifth Circuit noted in *Shimberg,* "[t]he theory behind tax-free corporate reorganizations is that the transaction is merely 'a continuance of the proprietary interests in the continuing enterprise under modified corporate form.' Lewis v. Commissioner of Internal Revenue, 176 F.2d 646, 648 (1 Cir.1949); Treas.Reg. § 1.368–1(b). See generally Cohen, *Conglomerate Mergers and Taxation,* 55 A.B.A.J. 40 (1969)." 577 F.2d at 288. As a result, the boot-for-stock transaction can be viewed as a partial repurchase of stock by the continuing corporate enterprise—i.e., as a redemption. It is of course true that both the pre- and post-reorganization analogies are somewhat artificial in that they imagine that the redemption occurred outside the confines of the actual reorganization. However, if forced to choose between the two analogies, the post-reorganization view is the less artificial. Although both analogies "recast the merger transaction," the post-reorganization view recognizes that a reorganization has taken place, while the pre-reorganization approach recasts the transaction to the exclusion of the overall exchange.

Moreover, we doubt that abandoning the pre- and post-reorganization analogies and the principles of § 302 in favor of a less artificial understanding of the transaction would lead to a result different from that reached by the Court of Appeals. Although the statute is admittedly ambiguous and the legislative history sparse, we are persuaded—even without relying on § 302—that Congress did not intend to except reorganizations such as that at issue here from the general rule allowing capital gains treatment for cash boot. 26 U.S.C. § 356(a)(1). The legislative history of § 356(a)(2), although perhaps generally "not illuminating," *Estate of Bedford,* 325 U.S., at 290, suggests that Congress was primarily concerned with preventing corporations from "siphon[ing] off" accumulated earnings and profits at a capital gains rate through the ruse of a reorganization. See Golub, 58 Taxes, at 905. This purpose is not served by denying capital gains treatment in a case such as this in which the taxpayer entered into an arm's length transaction with a corporation in which he had no prior interest, exchanging his stock in the acquired corporation for less than a one percent interest in the acquiring corporation and a substantial cash boot.

Section 356(a)(2) finds its genesis in § 203(d)(2) of the Revenue Act of 1924. See 43 Stat. 257. Although modified slightly over the years, the provisions are in relevant substance identical. The accompanying House Report asserts that § 203(d)(2) was designed to "preven[t] evasion." H.R.Rep. No. 179, 68th Cong., 1st Sess. 15 (1924). Without further explication, both the House and Senate Reports simply rely on an example to explain, in the words of both Reports, "[t]he necessity for this provision." Ibid; S.Rep. No. 398, 68th Cong., 1st Sess., 16 (1924). Significantly, the example describes a situation in which there was no change in the stockholders' relative ownership interests, but merely the creation of a wholly owned subsidiary as a mechanism for making a cash distribution to the shareholders:

> "Corporation A has capital stock of $100,000, and earnings and profits accumulated since March 1, 1913, of $50,000. If it distributes the $50,000 as a dividend to its stockholders, the amount distributed will be taxed at the full surtax rates.

> "On the other hand, Corporation A may organize Corporation B, to which it transfers all its assets, the consideration for the transfer being the issuance by B of all its stock and $50,000 in cash to the stockholders of Corporation A in exchange for their stock in Corporation A. Under the existing law, the $50,000 distributed with the stock of Corporation B would be taxed, not as a dividend, but as a capital gain, subject only to the 12½ per cent rate. The effect of such a distribution is obviously the same as if the corporation had declared out as a dividend its $50,000 earnings and profits. If dividends are to be subject to the full surtax rates, then such an amount so distributed should also be subject to the surtax rates and

not to the 12½ per cent rate on capital gain." Id., at 16; H.R.Rep. No. 179, at 15.

The "effect" of the transaction in this example is to transfer accumulated earnings and profits to the shareholders without altering their respective ownership interests in the continuing enterprise.

Of course, this example should not be understood as exhaustive of the proper applications of § 356(a)(2). It is nonetheless noteworthy that neither the example, nor any other legislative source, evinces a congressional intent to tax boot accompanying a transaction that involves a bona fide exchange between unrelated parties in the context of a reorganization as though the payment was in fact a dividend. To the contrary, the purpose of avoiding tax evasion suggests that Congress did not intend to impose an ordinary income tax in such cases. Moreover, the legislative history of § 302 supports this reading of § 356(a)(2) as well. In explaining the "essentially equivalent to a dividend" language of § 302(b)(1)—language that is certainly similar to the "has the effect ... of a dividend" language of § 356(a)(2)—the Senate Finance Committee made clear that the relevant inquiry is "whether or not the transaction by its nature may properly be characterized as a sale of stock ...." S.Rep. No. 1622, 83d Cong., 2d Sess., 234 (1954); cf. United States v. Davis, 397 U.S., at 311.

Examining the instant transaction in light of the purpose of § 356(a)(2), the boot-for-stock exchange in this case "may properly be characterized as a sale of stock." Significantly, unlike traditional single corporation redemptions and unlike reorganizations involving commonly owned corporations, there is little risk that the reorganization at issue was used as a ruse to distribute dividend. Rather, the transaction appears in all respects relevant to the narrow issue before us to have been comparable to an arm's length sale by the taxpayer to NL. This conclusion, moreover, is supported by the findings of the Tax Court. The court found that "[t]here is not the slightest evidence that the cash payment was a concealed distribution from BASIN." 86 T.C., at 155. As the Tax Court further noted, Basin lacked the funds to make such a distribution:

"Indeed, it is hard to conceive that such a possibility could even have been considered, for a distribution of that amount was not only far in excess of the accumulated earnings and profits ($2,319,611), but also of the total assets of BASIN ($2,758,069). In fact, only if one takes into account unrealized appreciation in the value of BASIN's assets, including good will and/or going concern value, can one possibly arrive at $3,250,000. Such a distribution could only be considered as the equivalent of a complete liquidation of BASIN ...." Ibid.[10]

In this context, even without relying on § 302 and the post-reorganization analogy, we conclude that the boot is better characterized as a part of the proceeds of a sale of stock than as a proxy for a dividend. As such, the payment qualifies for capital gains treatment.

The judgment of the Court of Appeals is accordingly

Affirmed.

Justice WHITE, dissenting: The question in this case is whether the cash payment of $3,250,000 by N.L. Industries, Inc. (NL) to Donald Clark, which he received in the April 18, 1979, merger of Basin Surveys, Inc. (Basin), into N.L. Acquisition Corporation (NLAC), had the effect of a distribution of a dividend under the Internal Revenue Code, 26 U.S.C. § 356(a)(2), to the extent of Basin's accumulated undistributed earnings and profits. Petitioner, the Commissioner of Internal Revenue (Commissioner) made this determination, taxing the sum as ordinary income, to find a 1979 tax deficiency of $972,504.74. The Court of Appeals disagreed, stating that because the cash payment resembles a hypothetical stock redemption from NL to Clark, the amount is taxable as capital gain. 828 F.2d 221 (CA–4 1987). Because the majority today agrees with that characterization, in spite of Clark's explicit refusal of the stock-for-stock exchange imagined by the Court of Appeals and the majority today, and because the record demonstrates, instead, that the transaction before us involved a boot distribution that had "the effect of the distribution of a dividend" under § 356(a)(2)—hence properly alerted the Commissioner to Clark's tax deficiency—I dissent.

The facts are stipulated. Basin, Clark, NL, and NLAC executed an Agreement and Plan of Merger dated April 3, 1979, which provided that on April 18, 1979, Basin would merge with NLAC. The statutory merger, which occurred pursuant to §§ 368(a)(1)(A) and (a)(2)(D) of the Code, and therefore qualified for tax-free reorganization status under § 354(a)(1), involved the following terms: Each outstanding share of NLAC stock remained outstanding; each outstanding share of Basin common stock was exchanged for $56,034.482 cash and 5,172.4137 shares of NL common stock; and each share of Basin common stock held by Basin was canceled. NLAC's name was amended to Basin Surveys, Inc. The Secretary of State of West Virginia certified that the merger complied with West Virginia law. Clark, the owner of all 58 outstanding shares of Basin, received $3,250,000 in cash and 300,000

---

10. The Commissioner maintains that Basin "could have distributed a dividend in the form of its own obligation (see, e.g., I.R.C. § 312(a)(2)) or it could have borrowed funds to distribute a dividend." Reply Brief for the United States 7. Basin's financial status, however, is nonetheless strong support for the Tax Court's conclusion that the cash payment was not a concealed dividend.

shares of NL stock. He expressly refused NL's alternative of 425,000 shares of NL common stock without cash. See App. 56–59.

Congress enacted § 354(a)(1) to grant favorable tax treatment to specific corporate transactions (reorganizations) that involve the exchange of stock or securities solely for other stock or securities. See Paulsen v. Commissioner, 469 U.S. 131, 136 (1985) (citing Treas.Reg. § 1.368–1(b), 26 CFR § 1.368–1(b) (1984), and noting the distinctive feature of such reorganizations, namely continuity-of-interests). Clark's "triangular merger" of Basin into NL's subsidiary NLAC qualified as one such tax-free reorganization, pursuant to § 368(a)(2)(D). Because the stock-for-stock exchange was supplemented with a cash payment, however, § 356(a)(1) requires that "the gain, if any, to the recipient shall be recognized, but in an amount not in excess of the sum of such money and the fair market value of such other property." Because this provision permitted taxpayers to withdraw profits during corporate reorganizations without declaring a dividend, Congress enacted the present § 356(a)(2), which states that when an exchange has "the effect of the distribution of a dividend," boot must be treated as a dividend, and taxed as ordinary income, to the extent of the distributee's "ratable share of the undistributed earnings and profits of the corporation ...." Ibid.; see also H.R.Rep. No. 179, 68th Cong., 1st Sess., 15 (1924) (illustration of § 356(a)(2)'s purpose to frustrate evasion of dividend taxation through corporate reorganization distributions); S.Rep. No. 398, 68th Cong., 1st Sess., 16 (1924) (same).

Thus the question today is whether the cash payment to Clark had the *effect* of a distribution of a dividend. We supplied the straightforward answer in United States v. Davis, 397 U.S. 301, 306, 312 (1970), when we explained that a pro rate redemption of stock by a corporation is "essentially equivalent" to a dividend. A pro rata distribution of stock, with no alteration of basic shareholder relationships, is the hallmark of a dividend. This was precisely Clark's gain. As sole shareholder of Basin, Clark necessarily received a pro rata distribution of monies that exceeded Basin's undistributed earnings and profits of $2,319,611. Because the merger and cash obligation occurred simultaneously on April 18, 1979, and because the statutory merger approved here assumes that Clark's proprietary interests continue in the restructured NLAC, the exact source of the pro rata boot payment is immaterial, which truth Congress acknowledged by requiring only that an exchange have the *effect* of a dividend distribution.

To avoid this conclusion, the Court of Appeals—approved by the majority today—recast the transaction as though the relevant distribution involved a single corporation's (NL's) stock redemption, which dividend equivalency is determined according to § 302 of the Code. Section 302 shields distributions from dividend taxation if the cash redemption is accompanied by sufficient loss of a shareholder's percentage interest in the corporation. The Court of Appeals hypothesized that Clark completed a pure stock-for-stock reorganization, receiving 425,000 NL shares, and thereafter redeemed 125,000 of these shares for his cash earnings of $3,250,000. The sum escapes dividend taxation because Clark's interest in NL theoretically declined from 1.3% to 0.92%, adequate to trigger § 302(b)(2) protection. Transporting § 302 from its purpose to frustrate shareholder sales of equity back to their own corporation, to § 356(a)(2)'s reorganization context, however, is problematic. Neither the majority nor the Court of Appeals explains why § 302 should obscure the core attribute of a dividend as a pro rata distribution to a corporation's shareholders;[1] nor offers insight into the mechanics of valuing hypothetical stock transfers and equity reductions; nor answers the Commissioner's observations that the sole shareholder of an acquired corporation will always have a smaller interest in the continuing enterprise when cash payments combine with a stock exchange. Last, the majority and the Court of Appeals' recharacterization of market happenings describes the exact stock-for-stock exchange, without a cash supplement, that Clark refused when he agreed to the merger.

Because the parties chose to structure the exchange as a tax-free reorganization under § 354(a)(1), and because the pro rata distribution to Clark of $3,250,000 during this reorganization had the *effect* of a dividend under § 356(a)(2), I dissent.[2]

Page 502:

Add to the facts of the Problem:

Prior to the acquisition of T, A had 500,000 shares of voting common stock outstanding (value—$10 per share). In each alternative below, A

---

[1]. The Court of Appeals' zeal to excoriate the "automatic dividend rule" leads to an opposite rigidity an automatic nondividend rule, even for pro rata boot payments. Any significant cash payment in a stock-for-stock exchange distributed to a sole shareholder of an acquired corporation will automatically receive capital gains treatment. Section 356(a)(2)'s exception for such payments that have attributes of a dividend disappears. Congress did not intend to handicap the Commissioner and courts with either absolute; instead, § 356(a)(1) instructs courts to make fact-specific inquiries into whether boot distributions accompanying corporate reorganizations occur on a pro rata basis to shareholders of the acquired corporation, and thus threaten a bailout of the transferor corporation's earnings and profits escaping a proper dividend tax treatment.

[2]. The majority's alternative holding that no statutory merger occurred at all—rather a taxable sale—is difficult to understand: All parties stipulate to the merger, which, in turn, was approved under West Virginia law; and Congress endorsed exactly such tax-free corporate transactions pursuant to its § 368(a)(1) reorganization regime. However apt the speculated sale analogy may be, if the April 3 Merger Agreement amounts to a sale of Clark's stock to NL, and not the intended merger, Clark would be subject to taxation on his full gain of over $10 million. The fracas over tax treatment of the cash boot would be irrelevant.

issued a total of 40,000 new shares of voting common stock (value—$400,000) in connection with the acquisition of T.

Page 503:

Delete the material in subsection (2) (pages 503–506) and insert:

3. CONSEQUENCES TO THE TARGET CORPORATION

Code: §§ 336(c); 357(a), (b), (c)(1); 358(a), (b)(1), (f); 361.
Regulations: § 1.357–1(a).

Treatment of the Reorganization Exchange. Without a nonrecognition provision, the target corporation in an acquisitive reorganization would realize gain or loss on the transfer of its assets and the assumption of its liabilities by the acquiring corporation. If the acquisition qualifies as a reorganization, however, Section 361(a) generally comes to the rescue by providing that the target recognizes no gain or loss if it exchanges property, pursuant to the reorganization plan, solely for stock or securities in a corporation which also is a party to the reorganization. Section 357(a) offers similar protection by providing generally that the assumption of the target's liabilities in a reorganization exchange will not be treated as boot nor prevent the exchange from being tax-free under Section 361(a).[1] These rules apply primarily to Type A and C reorganizations and forward triangular mergers. In a Type B stock-for-stock exchange or a reverse triangular merger, no assets are transferred because the target corporation remains intact as a controlled subsidiary of the acquiring corporation.

The target in a Type C reorganization may receive a limited amount of boot without disqualifying the transaction under Section 368.[2] In that event, the target must recognize any realized gain (but may not recognize loss) on the reorganization exchange to the extent of the cash and the fair market value of the boot that the target does not distribute pursuant to the plan of reorganization.[3] The target recognizes no gain on the reorganization exchange if it distributes all the boot it receives.[4] Any transfer by the target of cash or other boot received in the exchange to creditors in connection with the reorganization is treated

---

1. As in the Section 351 incorporation area, the general nonrecognition rule in Section 357(a) is subject to an exception in Section 357(b) if the liability assumption is motivated by tax avoidance or lacks a bona fide business purpose. The Section 357(c) exception for liabilities assumed in excess of the basis of the transferred assets only applies to a Type D reorganization. See infra Chapters 11 and 12.

2. I.R.C. § 368(a)(2)(B). Boot in a Type C reorganization would include any property other than stock or securities of the acquiring corporation (or its parent). See Section B3 of this Chapter (main text), infra.

3. I.R.C. § 361(b)(1)(B), (b)(2).

4. I.R.C. § 361(b)(1)(A).

as a "distribution" pursuant to the reorganization plan.[5] Since the target in a Type C reorganization is generally required to distribute all of its properties pursuant to the plan, gain or loss rarely will be recognized on the exchange.[6]

The protection afforded by Section 361(a) only applies to the *receipt* of boot by the target pursuant to the reorganization plan. An acquiring corporation that transfers appreciated boot property to the target as partial consideration for the target's assets must recognize gain under Section 1001 because, to that extent, the transaction is considered to be a taxable exchange.[7] In that event, the target takes the boot property with a fair market value basis.[8]

Treatment of Distributions. Following enactment of the 1986 Act, the tax treatment of distributions by the target in a reorganization raised some nettlesome technical questions thanks to the inept redrafting of Section 361.[9] TAMRA cleared up most of the confusion by adding new Section 361(c), which generally provides that a corporation does not recognize gain or loss on the distribution of "qualified property" to its shareholders pursuant to a reorganization plan. "Qualified property" is: (1) stock (or rights to acquire stock) in, or obligations (e.g., bonds and notes) of the distributing corporation, or (2) stock (or rights to acquire stock) in, or obligations of, another party to the reorganization which were received by the distributing corporation in the exchange. Thus, any stock, securities or even short-term notes of the acquiring corporation received by the target in the exchange and then distributed to its shareholders would constitute "qualified property." Section 361(c)(3) makes it clear that a transfer of "qualified property" by a target to its creditors in satisfaction of corporate liabilities is treated as a "distribution" pursuant to the reorganization plan.

If the target distributes an asset other than qualified property, it must recognize gain (but may not recognize loss) in the same manner as if the property had been sold to the distributee at its fair market value.[10] For example, the target would recognize gain on the distribution of appreciated retained assets (i.e., assets not acquired in the reorganization) or boot (other than notes of the acquiring corporation)

---

5. I.R.C. § 361(b)(3). The Service may prescribe regulations as necessary to prevent tax avoidance through abuse of this rule. Id.

6. A rare situation where gain could be recognized is where liabilities of the target are assumed in a transaction to which Section 357(b) or (c) applies.

7. Rev.Rul. 72–327 at p. 508 of the main text. Section 361(a) does not apply in this situation because it only provides nonrecognition to the *recipient* of boot.

8. I.R.C. § 358(a)(2). See also I.R.C. § 358(f).

9. For those who wish to revisit the muddle, see pages 504–505 of the main text. For a critique of the muddle, see Eustice, "A Case Study in Technical Tax Reform: Section 361, or How Not to Revise a Statute," 35 Tax Notes 283 (April 20, 1987).

10. I.R.C. § 361(c)(1), (2).

which appreciated between the time it was received and the distribution to shareholders.[11]

Sales Prior to Liquidation. Before liquidating, the target corporation in a Type C reorganization may sell some of the stock or securities received from the acquiring corporation in order to raise money to pay off creditors. Prior to the Tax Reform Act of 1986, the courts were divided over whether these sales were entitled to nonrecognition treatment.[12] The Fifth Circuit, concluding that the liquidation and reorganization provisions could work in tandem, held that sales made pursuant to a plan of complete liquidation were entitled to nonrecognition of gain under the 1954 Code version of Section 337.[13] For a time after the 1986 Act, it appeared that Congress may have accepted the result in this case (while rejecting its rationale) when it provided, in a now repealed version of Section 361, that the target would not recognize gain or loss on any "disposition" of stock or securities of the acquiring corporation received pursuant to the reorganization plan.[14] It appeared at the time that the target would not recognize gain or loss if it sold some of the acquiring corporation's stock or securities to pay off creditors, at least if the sale were "pursuant to the reorganization plan," but it would recognize gain or loss if it sold any retained property (i.e., property not acquired in the reorganization) or boot that appreciated after it was received from the acquiring corporation. Under current Section 361, however, only transfers of "qualified property" (i.e., stock or obligations of the acquiring corporation) or boot directly to creditors will qualify for nonrecognition.[15] Sales of property to third parties do not qualify for nonrecognition, even if the sales were necessary to raise money to pay off creditors.

Basis and Holding Period. If the target corporation retains property received from the acquiring corporation, which only could occur in a Type C reorganization where the Commissioner waives the Section 368(a)(2)(G) distribution requirement, it is deemed to have distributed that property to its shareholders, who then are treated as having recontributed the property to a "new" corporation as a contribution to

---

11. Since the target takes a fair market value basis in the boot under Section 358(a)(2) at the time of the exchange, it would recognize only post-acquisition appreciation on a later distribution of the boot.

12. Compare General Housewares Corp. v. United States, 615 F.2d 1056 (5th Cir. 1980) (allowing nonrecognition under former § 337) with FEC Liquidating Corp. v. United States, 548 F.2d 924 (Ct.Cl.1977) (taxing such gains on the ground that former § 337 and the reorganization provisions were conceptually incompatible).

13. General Housewares Corp. v. United States, supra note 10. Former Section 337 generally provided that a liquidating corporation did not recognize gain or loss on sales of assets pursuant to a plan of complete liquidation.

14. I.R.C. § 361(b)(3) (pre–1988).

15. I.R.C. § 361(b)(3), (c)(3).

capital.[16] The basis and the holding period of the property in the hands of the "new" corporation depend upon the consequences to the shareholders. If the property is boot to the shareholders, it receives a fair market value basis and no tacked holding period to either the shareholders or the "new" corporation to which it is constructively recontributed.[17] If the property is nonrecognition property (e.g., stock or securities of the acquiring corporation) to the shareholders, then their exchanged bases and tacked holding periods transfer to the "new" corporation.[18] These basis and holding period rules are irrelevant in the typical Type C reorganization where the target liquidates and distributes the stock, securities and boot received in the transaction, along with any retained assets, to its shareholders. In that event, the focus shifts to the operative provisions governing shareholders and security holders.[19]

16. See note 10 at page 476 of the main text.
17. I.R.C. §§ 358(a)(2); 362(a).
18. I.R.C. §§ 358(a)(1); 362(a); 1223(1) and (2).
19. See page 488 of the main text.

CHAPTER 11. NONACQUISITIVE, NONDIVISIVE REORGANIZATIONS

A. TYPE E: RECAPITALIZATIONS

Page 532:

Omit all the material under subsection (3) (pages 533–541) and insert:

The estate freezing advantages of a recapitalization discussed in the main volume have been eliminated by the enactment of Section 2036(c) in the 1987 Act. Under that section, which was revised by TAMRA, if a person holds a substantial (more than 10 percent) interest in an enterprise (e.g., Elder in the example in the text) and, after December 17, 1987, transfers property having a disproportionately large share of the potential appreciation in that person's interest in a business (e.g., common stock) enterprise while retaining an interest in the the income of the enterprise (e.g., preferred stock), then the retained interest will be treated as a retention of the enjoyment of the transferred property, rendering that property includible in the transferor's gross estate.

CHAPTER 12. CORPORATE DIVISIONS

B. THE REQUIREMENTS FOR A TAX–FREE CORPORATE DIVISION

Page 569:

After the second full paragraph, add:

After only 12 years of waiting, the Treasury finally promulgated final regulations under Section 355 in January, 1989. The final regulations, which in some instances go beyond the 1977 proposals, apply to transactions occurring after February 6, 1989. In the revisions below, the 1989 regulations have been fully integrated into the textual discussion.

Delete the Proposed Regulations assignment, and insert:

Regulations: § 1.355–1(b), –3.

Pages 583–586:

Delete the entire Note, and insert:

NOTE

Although the anti-bailout objective of the active business requirement is clear enough, this multifaceted test has engendered considerable litigation. The *Lockwood* case is typical of the Commissioner's unsuccessful early efforts to apply the test strictly. The Service retreated on a number of controversial issues in the 1977 proposed regulations, and most of these concessions were retained in the final regulations issued in 1989. This Note surveys some settled and lingering questions.

Trade or Business. Both the distributing corporation and the controlled corporation (or the controlled corporations in the case of a split-up) must be engaged immediately after the distribution in a trade or business with a five-year history. The regulations treat a corporation as being engaged in a trade or business if: [1]

> * * * a specific group of activities are being carried on by the corporation for the purpose of earning income or profit, and the activities included in such group include every operation that forms a part of, or a step in, the process of earning income or profit. Such group of activities ordinarily must include the collection of income and the payment of expenses.

---

1. Reg. § 1.355–3(b)(2)(ii).

The regulations go on to create a dichotomy between active and passive activities. Although the determination of whether a trade or business is "actively conducted" is a factual question turning on all the facts and circumstances, active business status generally requires the corporation to itself perform active and substantial management and operational functions.[2] For this purpose, the activities performed by persons outside the corporation, such as independent contractors, generally are not taken into account.[3] To preclude a tax-free separation of passive investment assets, "active conduct" does not include the holding of property for investment (e.g., raw land or portfolio securities) or the ownership and operation (including leasing) of real or personal property used in the owner's trade or business unless the owner performs significant management services with respect to the property.[4]

Vertical Divisions of a Single Integrated Business. Suppose a corporation wishes to divide a single trade or business that has been operated for more than five years? Does Section 355 require two separate predistribution trades or businesses, each with its own five year history, or may one existing business be divided in two? After several defeats,[5] the Service now acknowledges that Section 355 can apply to the separation of a single business. Thus, for example, assuming the other statutory requirements are met, a corporation engaged in an integrated business at one location may transfer half of its assets to a new subsidiary and distribute the stock of the subsidiary to a 50 percent shareholder in a tax-free split-off.[6]

Functional Divisions. The treatment of functional divisions—i.e., separations of certain distinct functions of a single business enterprise—is more uncertain. To illustrate the issue, assume that a manufacturer of high technology equipment wishes to spin off its research and development function for valid business reasons. The Service once maintained that such support activities did not constitute a separate trade or business because they did not independently produce income.[7] The regulations now sanction some types of functional divisions, as illustrated in the following example: [8]

Example (9). For the past eight years, corporation X has engaged in the manufacture and sale of household products. Through-

---

2. Reg. § 1.355–3(b)(2)(iii). Some of the corporation's activities, however, can be performed by others. Id.

3. Id.

4. Reg. § 1.355–3(b)(2)(iv).

5. See Coady v. Commissioner, 33 T.C. 771 (1960), affirmed per curiam 289 F.2d 490 (6th Cir.1961) (single construction business divided into two businesses to resolve shareholder dispute); United States v. Marett, 325 F.2d 28 (5th Cir.1963) (food manufacturer operating at three factories spun off one factory opened eight months before the distribution).

6. See, e.g., Reg. § 1.355–3(c) Examples (4) and (5).

7. Reg. § 1.355–1(c)(3) (pre–1989).

8. Reg. § 1.355–3(c) Example (9).

out this period, X has maintained a research department for use in connection with its manufacturing activities. The research department has 30 employees actively engaged in the development of new products. X transfers the research department to new subsidiary Y and distributes the stock of Y to X's shareholders. After the distribution, Y continues its research operations on a contractual basis with several corporations, including X. X and Y both satisfy the requirements of section 355(b). * * * The result in this example is the same if, after the distribution, Y continues its research operations but furnishes its services only to X. * * *

Similarly, if a steel manufacturer spins off a coal mine operated solely to supply its coal requirements, the manufacturing and captive coal mine activities will qualify as separate active businesses after the distribution.[9]

The 1989 regulations make it clear that the functional separation in the example above satisfies the active business test whether the research department subsequently provides services only to the business from which it was separated or also to other customers. The coal mine also was treated as an active business even though it did not derive income from outside third parties. These examples reflect the Service's abandonment of any requirement that an active business must "independently" produce income. But tax-free treatment for a functional division is still far from assured. The transaction also must have a corporate business purpose, and it must not run afoul of the "device" limitation. As we will discover shortly, the regulations provide that the same functional separations which pass muster under the active business test may present "evidence" of a prohibited bailout device.[10]

Geographical Divisions. The liberal approach of the *Lockwood* case has been incorporated into the final regulations. Previously, the Service applied a strict geographic test under which, for example, a manufacturer with factories in two locations could not separate out one plant unless they both had a five year business history. The current regulations dispense with geography and look to the character of the activity and commonality of functions in determining whether geographically dispersed operations constitute a single integrated business. Thus, a new activity in the same line of business as an activity that has been actively conducted by the distributing corporation for more than five years ordinarily will not be considered a separate business. For example, the regulations would permit a nine year old department store to spin off a suburban branch constructed three years ago, where

---

9. Reg. § 1.355–3(c) Example (11). See also Reg. § 1.355–3(c) Example (10), providing that the separation of the processing and sales functions of a meat products business satisfies the active business test.

10. See Reg. § 1.355–2(d)(2)(iv)(C).

after the distribution each store has its own manager and is operated independently of the other store.[11]

Single or Multiple Businesses. Section 355 requires that an active trade or business must have been actively conducted for the five years prior to the distribution and may not have been acquired within that period in a transaction that is taxable to the seller of the business.[12] The purpose of this requirement is to prevent a corporation from using Section 355 to avoid the dividend provisions of Subchapter C by temporarily investing its earnings in a business that it plans to spin off to its shareholders.

The five year rule has spawned numerous controversies over whether a particular activity is a separate business requiring its own five year history or simply part of an integrated business which has been active for more than five years. We have seen, for example, that a recently opened suburban branch store may be treated as an integral part of an ongoing department store business with a more than five year history.[13] On the other hand, businesses with clearly distinct products or services (e.g., a chicken ranch and a winery) are considered to be separate.[14] As *Lockwood* illustrates, similar problems arise in the case of a diversification or expansion of a business within the five year predistribution period. The 1989 regulations offer some guidance on this question, suggesting that a newer activity in the same line of business will be treated as an expansion of the original business unless the "purchase, creation, or other acquisition effects a change of such a character as to constitute the acquisition of a new or different business."[15] Revenue Ruling 59–400, which follows this Note in the main volume, addresses yet another aspect of this problem—the situation where the earnings of one business are used to finance the growth of a newer enterprise.

Real Estate. The Service has consistently maintained that investment land or owner-occupied real estate ordinarily do not constitute actively conducted businesses.[16] The 1989 regulations provide that the separation of owner-occupied real estate will be subject to "careful scrutiny;" real estate qualifies as an active business only if the owner performs "significant services with respect to the operation and

---

11. Reg. § 1.355–3(c) Example (7). See also Reg. § 1.355–3(c) Example (8), illustrating the same result where the new activity is purchased as a going concern.

12. I.R.C. § 355(b)(2). For this purpose, a "taxable transaction" is one in which gain or loss was recognized by the seller. If a business is acquired in a tax-free reorganization, its previous history carries over (along with its tax attributes) for purposes of the five year rule.

13. Reg. § 1.355–3(c) Example (7).

14. See, e.g., Rev.Rul. 56–655, 1956–2 C.B. 214 (retail appliance branch and retail furniture branch considered separate businesses); Rev.Rul. 56–451, 1956–2 C.B. 208 (metal industry magazine separate from magazine to serve electrical industry).

15. Reg. § 1.355–3(b)(3)(ii).

16. Reg. § 1.355–3(b)(2)(iv).

management of the property."[17] Thus, the Service will not approve the spin-off of vacant land or mineral rights on ranch land, even if development activities are imminent.[18] But it will sanction the separation of an office building substantially leased (10 of 11 floors) to outsiders and actively managed by the lessor.[19] Even if the active business hurdle is surmounted, however, separations of real estate may be vulnerable under the "device" and business purpose tests.[20]

Dispositions of Recently Acquired Businesses. Congress added another requirement to the active trade or business test in the 1987 Act as part of its effort to preclude a corporation from disposing of a recently acquired division or subsidiary without paying a corporate-level tax. As amended, Section 355(b)(2)(D) provides that a distribution will flunk the active trade or business test if control of the *distributing* corporation was acquired by a corporate distributee within the five-year period preceding the distribution. For this purpose, all members of an affiliated group of corporations are treated as a single corporate distributee.

The problem at which this amendment is directed is where one corporation ("P") acquires all the stock of a target ("T") which is directly engaged in the active conduct of a trade or business and also owns the stock of a subsidiary ("S") similarly engaged, both businesses having more than five year histories. If P wished to dispose of the S business without recognition of the gain inherent in S's assets, it could cause T to distribute the stock of S to P in a tax-free Section 355 distribution. The Service had ruled that such a distribution qualified as tax-free where P purchased T with an S subsidiary having a five year business history, and T thereafter distributed the S stock to P; the distribution did not violate the active trade or business requirement unless P attempted a bailout by distributing the S stock to its shareholders.[21] P then would allocate its cost basis in the stock of recently purchased T between T and S under Section 358, obtaining a fair market value basis in the stock of both businesses. As the final step, P would sell the S stock without recognition of any further gain. Under Section 355(b)(2)(D), as amended, the distribution of S stock would not qualify as tax-free because control of the distributing corporation (T) was acquired by a corporate distributee (P) within the five-year period preceding the distribution.

17. Id.

18. Reg. § 1.355–3(c) Examples (2) and (3).

19. Reg. § 1.355–3(c) Example (12). Compare Reg. § 1.355–3(c) Example (13), where the separation of a two-story office building did not qualify where the distributing corporation occupied the ground floor and half of the second floor in the conduct of its banking business and rented the remaining area as storage space.

20. See, e.g., Reg. § 1.355–2(d)(2)(iv)(C).

21. Rev.Rul. 74–5, 1974–1 C.B. 82. But query whether the subsequent sale of S stock would cause the transaction to violate the device limitation?

In its haste to meet the concern described above, however, Congress committed a drafting foot fault and repealed the long-standing anti-bailout rule (in pre–1987 Section 355(b)(2)(D)) prohibiting the distribution of stock of a corporation which had been acquired by the distributing corporation in a taxable transaction within the five year period preceding the distribution. TAMRA cured this inadvertent error by again amending Section 355(b)(2)(D) to make it clear that Section 355 does not generally apply if, within five years prior to the distribution, the distributing corporation acquires control, directly or indirectly, of a corporation which (at the time of the acquisition of control) is conducting the active trade or business of the distributing corporation or the controlled corporation.

Pages 589–592:

Delete the text under "4. THE DEVICE LIMITATION," and insert:

4. THE "DEVICE" LIMITATION

Code: § 355(a)(1)(B).

Regulations: § 1.355–2(d).

Section 355(a)(1)(B) provides that a corporate division may not be "used principally as a device for the distribution of the earnings and profits" of the distributing corporation or the controlled subsidiary. The historic mission of this requirement apparently was to prevent the conversion of ordinary dividend income into preferentially taxed capital gain through a bailout masquerading as a corporate division.[1] This goal is reaffirmed in the 1989 regulations, which remind us that:[2]

> * * * a tax-free distribution of the stock of a controlled corporation presents a potential for tax avoidance by facilitating the avoidance of the dividend provisions of the code through the subsequent sale or exchange of stock of one corporation and the retention of the stock of another corporation. A device can include a transaction that effects a recovery of basis.

The repeal of the capital gains preference in the Tax Reform Act of 1986 raised the question of whether the device requirement had waned in significance, perhaps to the vanishing point. If ordinary income and capital gains are taxed at the same rate, a bailout offers minimal potential to avoid tax at the shareholder level. But tax avoidance still might result from a transaction that effects a recovery of basis—for example, a spin-off followed by a subsequent sale of all or part of the controlled corporation's stock. The above excerpt from the 1989 regula-

---

1. See, e.g., Rev.Rul. 71–383, 1971–2 C.B. 180.

2. Reg. § 1.355–2(d)(1).

tions suggests as much and indicates that the Treasury will continue to invoke the device limitation even a regime without a capital gains preference.

Even before the uncertainty engendered by the 1986 tax reforms, the meaning and scope of the "device" limitation were mired in obscurity. The 1989 regulations initially fail to burn off the fog, declaring that "generally, the determination of whether a transaction was used principally as a device will be made from all of the facts and circumstances."[3] The regulations then offer some guidance by identifying certain "device" and "nondevice" factors which are "evidence" of the presence or absence of a device, but the strength of this "evidence" still depends on "the facts and circumstances."[4]

Transactions Ordinarily Not a Device. Notwithstanding the presence or absence of the "device factors" to be discussed below, the regulations identify three transactions that "ordinarily" are not considered a tax avoidance device. Distributions are presumed innocent if:

(1) the distributing and controlled corporations have neither accumulated nor current earnings and profits as of the date of the distribution, taking into account the possibility that a distribution by the distributing corporation would create earnings and profits if Section 355 did not apply;[5]

(2) in the absence of Section 355, the distribution would qualify as a redemption to pay death taxes under Section 303;[6] and

(3) in the absence of Section 355, the distribution would qualify, with respect to each distributee shareholder, as an exchange redemption under Section 302(a).[7]

Any of these distributions loses its protection, however, if it involves the distribution of the stock of more than one controlled corporation and facilitates the avoidance of the dividend provisions of the Code through the subsequent sale or exchange of stock of one corporation and the retention of the stock of another corporation.[8]

Device and Nondevice Factors: In General. The regulations specify three factors that are "evidence" of a device ("device factors") and three factors that are evidence of a nondevice ("nondevice factors"). The three device factors are: (1) a pro rata distribution; (2) a subsequent

---

3. Reg. § 1.355–2(d)(1).
4. Reg. § 1.355–2(d)(2)(i), (3)(i).
5. Reg. § 1.355–2(d)(5)(ii).
6. Reg. § 1.355–2(d)(5)(iii). See Chapter 5H of the main text, supra.
7. Reg. § 1.355–2(d)(5)(iv). For this purpose, the waiver of family attribution rules apply without regard to the ten year look forward rule and the requirement to file a waiver agreement in Sections 302(c)(2)(A)(ii) and (iii). See Chapter 5C of the main text, supra.
8. Reg. § 1.355–2(d)(5)(i). For an example, see Reg. § 1.355–2(d)(5)(v) Example (2).

sale or exchange of stock of either the distributing or controlled corporation; and (3) the nature and use of the assets of the distributing and controlled corporations immediately after the transaction.[9] The three nondevice factors are: (1) the corporate business purpose for the transaction; (2) the fact that the distributing corporation is publicly traded and widely held; and (3) the fact that the stock of the controlled corporation is distributed to one or more domestic corporations which would be entitled to a dividends received deduction under Section 243 if Section 355 does not apply to the transaction.[10] The presence of one or more of these factors is not controlling, however, and the "strength" of the evidence depends on the facts and circumstances.[11]

Pro Rata Distribution. A pro rata distribution—for example, a spin-off—is considered to present the greatest potential for avoidance of the dividend provisions of Subchapter C and thus is more likely to be used principally as a device. As a result, the regulations provide that a pro rata or substantially pro rata distribution is evidence of a device.[12]

Subsequent Sale or Exchange of Stock. A parenthetical clause in Section 355(a)(1)(B) cryptically provides that the "mere fact" that stock or securities of either the distributing or controlled corporations is sold by all or some of the shareholders is not to be construed to mean that the transaction was used principally as a device. But the Service has long contended that a sale of stock of the distributing or controlled corporation shortly after a corporate division is evidence that the transaction was used as bailout device. Under the 1989 regulations, the "strength" of the evidence depends upon the percentage of stock disposed of after the distribution, the length of time between the distribution and the subsequent sale and the extent to which the subsequent sale was prearranged.[13]

A subsequent sale or exchange negotiated or agreed upon before the distribution is "substantial evidence" of a device.[14] A sale is always prearranged if it was "pursuant to an arrangement negotiated or agreed upon before the distribution if enforceable rights to buy or sell existed before the distribution." [15] The regulations are more equivocal if a sale was merely discussed by the parties but was "reasonably to be

---

9. Reg. § 1.355–2(d)(2).
10. Reg. § 1.355–2(d)(3).
11. Reg. § 1.355–2(d)(2)(i); –2(d)(3)(i).
12. Reg. § 1.355–2(d)(2)(ii).
13. Reg. § 1.355–2(d)(2)(iii)(A).
14. Reg. § 1.355–2(d)(2)(iii)(B). In this respect, the 1989 regulations are more lenient than the 1977 proposals, under which a subsequent sale or exchange of 20 percent or more of the stock of either the distributing or controlled corporation, prearranged before the distribution, was conclusive evidence of a device. The final regulations drop the *per se* rule and allow taxpayers to prove that, despite the sale or exchange, the transaction was not used principally as a device.
15. Reg. § 1.355–2(d)(2)(iii)(D).

anticipated." In that event, it "ordinarily" will be considered to be previously negotiated or agreed upon.[16] Seemingly ignoring the express language of Section 355(a)(1)(B), the regulations also provide that even in the absence of prior negotiations or agreement, a subsequent sale nonetheless is "evidence of a device."[17]

The perceived bailout abuse of a subsequent sale normally occurs only when the selling shareholders cash out their investment. The regulations logically provide that if the shareholders dispose of stock in a subsequent tax-free reorganization in which no more than an "insubstantial" amount of gain is recognized, the transaction will not be treated as a subsequent sale or exchange. Rather, because the shareholders maintain an interest in the continuing enterprise, the stock received in the exchange is treated as the stock surrendered.[18] But any subsequent sale of the new stock received will be subject to the "subsequent sale" rules and could be evidence of a device.[19]

The Service's reliance on subsequent stock sales (whether or not prearranged) as substantial evidence of a device has always been questionable. To return to the introductory example in the main text, assume that Diverse Corporation has actively conducted profitable winery and chicken ranch businesses for more than five years. If Diverse wished to spin off the chicken ranch as Poultry, Inc., it would have no difficulty satisfying the active business test. But what if the spin-off were the prelude to a prearranged sale of the Poultry, Inc. stock by the controlling shareholders? If that sale were taxable to the shareholders at capital gains rates, or even if it merely effected a recovery of part of the shareholders' basis in their Diverse Corp. stock, should the spin-off be viewed principally as a device to bail out Diverse's earnings and profits?

In considering these questions, keep in mind the alternatives available to Diverse. If the corporation simply had sold the chicken ranch assets and distributed the proceeds to its noncorporate shareholders, the distribution likely would have qualified as a partial liquidation, entitling noncorporate shareholders to exchange treatment.[20] The same result would have occurred if the chicken ranch assets were distributed pro rata to the shareholders and sold shortly thereafter. To be sure, if the sale were consummated or prearranged by the corporation, it would have triggered gain at the corporate *and* shareholder

16. Id.
17. Reg. § 1.355–2(d)(2)(iii)(C).
18. Reg. § 1.355–2(d)(2)(iii)(E).
19. Id.

20. See I.R.C. § 302(b)(4), (e). But see Rev.Rul. 75–223, 1975–1 C.B. 109, at p. 221 of the main text, supra, in which the Service ruled that a distribution of stock of a subsidiary may not qualify as a partial

levels.[21] But, historically at least, the principal concern in Section 355 was not with the double taxation of corporate earnings but rather the tax treatment of a distribution to the shareholders. If an economically equivalent transaction (i.e., a partial liquidation) would have qualified for capital gain treatment, then it seems anomalous to classify a spin-off followed by a prearranged sale of the same business as a device to convert ordinary dividend income to capital gain. In the last analysis, the answer may be to treat partial liquidation distributions as dividends to noncorporate shareholders. Moreover, even if it is not a device, a distribution followed by a taxable sale is unlikely to satisfy the business purpose test and, if the sale closely follows the distribution but somehow escapes the device limitation, the transaction may fail the continuity of interest requirement.

Nature and Use of the Assets. The regulations also enforce the device limitation by taking into account the "nature, kind, amount, and use of the assets of the distributing and the controlled corporations (and corporations controlled by them) immediately after the transaction." [22] Thus, the existence of assets that are not used in an active trade or business, such as cash and other liquid assets that are not related to the reasonable needs of the active business, is evidence of a device.[23] To illustrate, assume that Corporation X spins off Corporation Y in order to comply with certain regulatory requirements under state law. As part of the separation, X transfers excess cash (not related to the reasonable needs of X or Y's business) to Y and then distributes the Y stock pro rata to X's shareholders. The result of this infusion of cash into Y is that the percentage of liquid assets not related to the trade or business is substantially greater for Y than for X. The regulations view this as suspect, providing in an example that the transfer of cash by X to Y is "relatively strong evidence of device." [24] When coupled with the pro rata nature of the distribution, the transaction is considered to have been used principally as a device notwithstanding the "strong business purpose" because there was no business purpose for the infusion of cash into Y.[25]

The regulations also consider the relationship between the distributing and controlled corporations and the effect of a sale of one of the businesses on the overall enterprise. Evidence of a device is presented

---

liquidation. See also Morgenstern v. Commissioner (1971) (Unpublished Case).

21. See Chapter 7 in the main text, supra.
22. Reg. § 1.355–2(d)(2)(iv).
23. Reg. § 1.355–2(d)(2)(iv)(A), (B).
24. Reg. § 1.355–2(d)(4) Example (3).
25. Reg. § 1.355–2(d)(2)(iv)(B); 1.355–2(d)(4) Example (3). Compare Reg.

§ 1.355–2(d)(4) Example (2), where the transfer of cash and liquid securities from the distributing to the controlled corporation was "relatively weak evidence of device" because after the transfer the two corporations held liquid assets in amounts proportional to the values of their businesses.

if the distributing or controlled corporation is a business that principally serves the business of the other corporation (a "secondary business") and it can be sold without adversely affecting the business of the other corporation.[26] Thus, the spin-off of a captive coal mine from a steel manufacturer, a transaction which satisfied the active business test,[27] nonetheless presents evidence of a device if the principal function of the coal mine is to satisfy the requirements of the steel business and the coal mine could be sold without adversely affecting the steel business.[28] The apparent concern here is not so much with the potential for tax avoidance through non-arm's length intercorporate transactions between the separated corporations; that type of abuse is adequately policed by Section 482, which authorizes the Commissioner to allocate income or deductions between or among commonly controlled trades or businesses. What appears to be bothering the Service is the likelihood for avoidance of the dividend provisions of the Code when the "related function" is not truly integral to the business from which it has been separated.

Nondevice Factors. Acknowledging that the corporate business purposes for a transaction may be sufficiently compelling to outweigh any evidence of a device, the regulations provide that the corporate business purpose for a transaction is evidence of nondevice.[29] In keeping with the "sliding scale" approach that pervades the device regulations, the stronger the evidence of device, then the stronger is the business purpose required to prevent determination that the transaction was used principally as a device.[30] The strength of a corporate business purpose, of course, is based on all the facts and circumstances, including but not limited to the importance of achieving the purpose to the success of the business, the extent to which the transaction is prompted by a person not having a proprietary interest in either corporation or by other outside factors beyond the control of the distributing corporation, and the "immediacy of the conditions" prompting the transaction.[31]

The fact that the distributing corporation is publicly traded and widely held, having no shareholder who directly or indirectly owns more than five percent of any class of stock, also is evidence of nondevice.[32]

26. Reg. § 1.355–2(d)(2)(C).

27. See Reg. § 1.355–3(c) Example (11).

28. Reg. § 1.355–2(d)(3)(C). Likewise, the separation of the sales and manufacturing functions will constitute evidence of a device if the principal function of the sales operation after the separation is to sell the output from the manufacturing operation and the sales operation could be sold without adversely affecting the manufacturing operation.

29. Reg. § 1.355–2(d)(3)(ii).

30. Id.

31. Id.

32. Reg. § 1.355–2(d)(3)(iii).

Finally, the fact that the stock of the controlled corporation is distributed to a domestic corporate distributee which, without Section 355, would be entitled to the Section 243 dividends received deduction, is evidence of a nondevice.[33]

Page 593:

Delete the Proposed Regulations assignment, and insert:

Regulations: § 1.355–2(b), (c).

Page 599:

Before the Note, insert:

REVENUE RULING 88–34
1988–1 Cum.Bull. 115.

ISSUE

Is the business purpose requirement of section 355 of the Internal Revenue Code and section 1.355–2(c) of the Income Tax Regulations met where a distribution of the stock of a controlled corporation is made to enable that corporation to hire a new president?

FACTS

X, a large widely held and publicly traded corporation, owned all the stock of Y corporation for more than five years. X and Y were each engaged in the active conduct of a separate and distinct trade or business for over five years. No shareholder of X owns as much as 5 percent of the outstanding stock of X.

The president of Y has recently retired and Y has conducted an extensive search for a new president. Y has interviewed A, an individual with substantial prior experience and an outstanding reputation as the president of a public corporation engaged in the same line of business as Y. Because of A's prior experience and success in managing a similar corporation, A is the person Y wishes to hire as its new president. A is interested in becoming the president of Y but will not accept the position unless permitted to acquire a significant equity interest in Y. A has further advised Y that A is not interested in acquiring X stock or in acquiring an equity interest in Y as a subsidiary of X.

In order to permit Y to obtain the services of A, X has distributed all of the stock of Y pro rata to the shareholders. Thereafter, A will be employed by Y at an annual salary of $250x and, within one year, will purchase newly issued shares of stock from Y having a fair market value of $775x.

---

33. Reg. § 1.355–2(d)(3)(iv).

Except for the issue of the business purpose for the distribution, the proposed distribution by X of the Y stock meets all the requirements of section 355 of the Code and the pertinent regulations.

LAW AND ANALYSIS

Section 355 of the Code provides that under certain circumstances a corporation may distribute stock or securities in a corporation it controls to its shareholders or security holders in a transaction that is not taxable to those shareholders or security holders. Section 1.355–2(c) of the regulations states that a distribution by a corporation of stock or securities of a controlled corporation will not qualify under section 355 when carried out for purposes not germane to the business of the corporations. This provision is intended to limit the application of section 355 to those readjustments of a corporate structure that are required by business exigencies.

Situation 2 of Rev.Rul. 69–460, 1969–2 C.B. 51, concerns a distribution of the stock of a subsidiary corporation so that key employees of the parent corporation could afford to buy stock in that corporation. That ruling holds that the distribution was undertaken for a valid business purpose. Rev.Rul. 85–127, 1985–2 C.B. 119, holds that the business purpose requirement was also met where a corporation transfers one of its businesses to a new corporation and distributes the stock of the new corporation to its shareholders in order to retain the services of a key employee and permit that employee to obtain a majority of the stock of the new corporation.

In the present situation, the distribution enables the subsidiary corporation to hire the key employee it believes is necessary to the continued success of the business. This is consistent with both Rev.Rul. 69–460 (Situation 2) and Rev.Rul. 85–127.

HOLDING

The pro rata distribution of the stock of Y by X to the X shareholders to enable Y to hire A as its new president is for a valid business purpose within the meaning of section 1.355–2(c) of the regulations. The distribution qualifies under section 355 of the Code because all other requirements of section 355 and the regulations thereunder have been met.

Pages 599–600:

Delete the Note, and insert:

NOTE

Business Purpose. The regulations acknowledge the close relationship between the business purpose and device requirements by providing that a corporate business purpose is "evidence" that a transaction was not used principally as a device.[1] But they nonetheless emphasize that the corporate business purpose for a division is an independent requirement. Thus, a transaction lacking a corporate business purpose will not qualify under Section 355 even if it is not used principally as a bailout device.[2] The regulations define a corporate business purpose as "a real and substantial non-Federal tax purpose germane to the business of the distributing corporation, the controlled corporation or the affiliated group to which the distributing corporation belongs."[3]

The 1989 regulations provide examples of valid and invalid corporate business purposes. Divisions motivated by the necessity to comply with an antitrust decree, to resolve shareholder disputes or even to permit shareholders to pursue separate interests are considered to be valid corporate business purposes.[4] A *shareholder* purpose normally does not suffice, but if a shareholder purpose for a transaction is so nearly coextensive with a corporate business purpose as to preclude any distinction between them, the transaction will pass muster.[5]

A business purpose will not exist if the same corporate objectives can be met through a nontaxable transaction that does not involve the distribution of stock of a controlled corporation and which is neither impractical nor unduly expensive.[6] For example, assume that a corporation manufactures both toys and candy through divisions which are not separately incorporated, and the shareholders wish to protect the candy business from the risks of the toy business. If that goal can be achieved by dropping down the assets of one of the businesses to a new subsidiary, a subsequent distribution of that stock to the parent's shareholders will not be carried out for a corporate business purpose.[7]

Continuity of Interest. The regulations require that those persons who owned an interest in the enterprise prior to the division must own, in the aggregate, an amount of stock establishing a continuity of interest in each of the modified corporate forms in which the enterprise is conducted after the Section 355 transaction.[8] Roughly translated, this means that the former owners of the distributing corporation must

---

1. Reg. § 1.355–2(b)(4). See also Reg. § 1.355–2(d)(3)(ii).

2. Reg. § 1.355–2(b)(1).

3. Reg. § 1.355–2(b)(2). The Service has ruled that the reduction of state and local taxes can be a corporate business purpose. Rev.Rul. 76–187, 1976–1 C.B. 97. But the 1989 regulations make it clear that a purpose of reducing "non Federal" taxes is not a corporate business purpose if: (1) the transaction will result in a reduction in both Federal and non Federal taxes because of similarities in the respective laws, and (2) the reduction of Federal taxes is greater than or substantially coextensive with the reduction of non Federal taxes. Reg. § 1.355–2(b)(1) and (2). See Reg. § 1.355–2(b)(5) Examples (6), (7) and (8).

4. Reg. § 1.355–2(a)(5) Examples (1) and (2).

5. Reg. § 1.355–2(b)(2).

6. Reg. § 1.355–2(b)(3).

7. Reg. § 1.355–2(b)(3), –2(b)(5) Example (3). See also Reg. § 1.355–2(b)(5) Examples (4) and (5).

8. Reg. § 1.355–2(c)(1).

emerge from the transaction (in the aggregate) with at least a 50 percent equity interest in each of the corporations resulting from the newly structured enterprise. Since the device limitation patrols against prearranged postdistribution sales, this additional judicial test seems superfluous, and the doctrine has been sparingly invoked in the context of a corporate division.[9] But the 1989 regulations emphasize that the continuity of interest requirement is independent of the other Section 355 tests.[10]

We have seen that one typical corporate division is a non pro rata distribution structured as a split-off or split-up, where a corporate enterprise is divided up to allow feuding shareholders to go their separate ways, each taking a piece of the business. The regulations acknowledge that this type of transaction satisfies the continuity of interest requirement because the prior owners of the integrated enterprise, in the aggregate, emerge with all the stock of the two corporations resulting from the separation.

Assume, however, that shareholders A and B each own 50 percent of the stock of X, Inc., which is engaged in one business, and X, Inc. owns all the stock of S, Inc., which is engaged in a different business. If new shareholder C purchases all of A's stock in X, Inc., and then X, Inc. distributes all the stock of S, Inc. to B in redemption of B's X, Inc. stock, the continuity of interest test will not be met because the owners of X, Inc. prior to the distribution do not, in the aggregate, own an amount of stock establishing continuity of interest in each of X and S after the distribution.[11] The smoking pistol is that A and B together did not own the minimum stock interest in X that would be required in order to maintain continuity of interest.[12] Without explicitly saying so, several examples in the regulations indicate that a 50 percent equity interest, the benchmark for acquisitive reorganizations,[13] is what is needed to "maintain" continuity of interest.[14]

9. For a rare published ruling on the application of the continuity of interest doctrine to a spin-off, see Rev.Rul. 79–273, 1979–2 C.B. 125, where the Service ruled that a distribution did not meet the continuity of interest doctrine where the distributing parent corporation subsequently was acquired in a reverse cash merger. Under the facts of the ruling, the distributing corporation was worth more than the controlled subsidiary, and thus the equity interest retained by the shareholders represented less than 50 percent in value of their original holdings.

10. Reg. § 1.355–2(c)(1).

11. Reg. § 1.355–2(c)(2) Example (3).

12. Id.

13. See Chapter 10B1a, supra, in the main text.

14. See, e.g., Reg. § 1.355–2(c)(2) Example (2), where C in the example in the text purchased only 50 percent of A's X, Inc. stock so that after the split-off, A and C each own 50 percent of X, Inc. and B owns 100 percent of S, Inc. The continuity of interest test is met here because one or more of the owners of X prior to the distribution own, in the aggregate, "an amount of stock establishing a continuity of interest in each of X and S after the distribution." Id.

Ch. 12   CORPORATE DIVISIONS

D. THE OPERATIVE PROVISIONS

Page 615:

Add to the Code assignment: § 355(c).

Pages 617–618:

Delete the final incomplete paragraph on page 617 and the first full paragraph on page 618, and insert:

Recognition of Gain or Loss to the Distributing Corporation. Section 355 itself only governs the tax consequences of a corporate division at the shareholder level. The tax consequences to the distributing corporation are determined by Section 361(c), if the distribution is coupled with a Type D reorganization, or by Section 355(c) if it is not.

If a Section 355 distribution is part of a reorganization plan, the distributing corporation does not recognize gain on the distribution of "qualified property"—i.e., stock or debt obligations of the controlled corporation—to its shareholders.[21] Thus, in the typical spin-off or split-off, where the distributing corporation's basis in the stock of the controlled corporation is normally less than its fair market value, no corporate-level gain is recognized on the distribution. Section 311(b), which otherwise might have required gain recognition, is not applicable because it only applies to distributions to which Subpart A of Subchapter C (Sections 301–307) applies, and Section 355 is not within Subpart A.[22] The same result would occur on a split-up; Section 336, which otherwise might have required gain to be recognized, does not apply to "reorganization" distributions.[23] Gain is recognized, however, on the distribution of appreciated boot in any Section 355 distribution that is part of a reorganization.[23A]

If a Section 355 distribution is not preceded by a Type D reorganization, Section 355(c) provides that no gain or loss will be recognized on a distribution of stock or securities in the controlled corporation.[23B] Gain

---

21. I.R.C. § 361(c)(1), (2).

22. See also I.R.C. § 361(c)(4).

23. I.R.C. § 361(c)(4); see also § 336(c).

23A. I.R.C. § 361(c)(2).

23B. The legislative history of TAMRA makes it clear that the gain recognition rule of Section 311(b) will *not* apply to the distribution of securities in a qualifying corporate division even if the recipient is taxed under Section 355(a)(3)(A) (i.e., where the principal amount of securities received exceeds the principal amount of any securities surrendered). Gain will be recognized, however, on the distribution of appreciated stock that is not permitted to be received tax-free by the shareholders. Staff of Joint Committee on Taxation, Description of Technical Corrections Bill of 1988, 100th Cong., 2d Sess. 386 (1988).

(but not loss) would be recognized under Section 311(b) on the distribution of any other property—e.g., appreciated boot.[23C]

[23C] Section 355(c) incorporates Section 311 by reference for this purpose, even in the case of split-up distributions, which otherwise would be governed by Section 336 in the absence of a reorganization.

CHAPTER 13. LIMITATIONS ON CARRYOVERS OF CORPORATE ATTRIBUTES

B. LIMITATIONS ON NET OPERATING LOSS CARRYFORWARDS: SECTION 382

Page 635:

After the first full paragraph, add:

TAMRA expanded the special rule in Section 382(e)(2) to include not only redemptions but also other corporate contractions. Congress concluded that the fact that a transaction may not constitute a "redemption" for other tax purposes should not determine its tax treatment under Section 382. For example, a "bootstrap" acquisition, in which aggregate corporate value is directly or indirectly reduced or burdened by debt to provide funds to the old shareholders, could be subject to Section 382(e)(2). Staff of Joint Committee on Taxation, Description of the Technical Corrections Bill of 1988, 100th Cong., 2d Sess. 44 (1988).

Page 636:

After the first full paragraph, add:

The 1987 Act amended Section 382(h)(2)(B) by expanding the definition of "recognized built-in loss" to include amounts allowable as depreciation, amortization or depletion for any period within the "recognition period" except to the extent that the "new loss corporation" establishes that these allowable amounts are not attributable to the excess of the adjusted basis of the corporation's assets over the fair market value of the asset on the "change date." The purpose of this mysterious new language is to make it clear that the special limitations on the use of built-in losses following an ownership change apply to built-in depreciation, amortization and depletion.

Add to footnote 33:

TAMRA clarified the treatment of built-in gain if a Section 338 election is made in connection with an ownership change. If the 25 percent built-in gain threshold (see I.R.C. § 382(h)(3)(B)) is not met with respect to the ownership change, the Section 382 limitation for the post-change year in which gain is recognized by reason of the Section 338 election is increased by the lesser of: (1) the amount of net unrealized built-in gain (determined as of the date of the ownership change, without regard to the 25 percent threshold requirement), or (2) the gain recognized by reason of Section 388. I.R.C. § 338(h)(1)(C).

Pages 638-641:

Section D should be retitled "OTHER LOSS LIMITATIONS," followed by "1. ACQUISITIONS MADE TO EVADE TAX: SECTION 269." The problem at page 641 should be deleted and the following should be added at the bottom of page 641:

2. LIMITATIONS ON USE OF PREACQUISITION LOSSES TO OFFSET BUILT-IN GAINS: SECTION 384

Code § 384.

Section 384 was added in the 1987 Act to restrict an acquiring corporation from using its preacquisition losses to offset built-in gains of an acquired corporation.

The policy and operation of Section 384 can best be illustrated by an example. Assume that Loss Corporation ("L") has $100,000 of net operating loss carryforwards. At the beginning of the current year, profitable Target Corporation ("T") merges into L in a tax-free Type A reorganization. L and T are owned by unrelated individual shareholders, and the merger does not result in a Section 382 ownership change to L. T's only asset, Gainacre, has a value of $200,000 and an adjusted basis of $125,000 which will transfer to L under Section 362(b). Assume that L sells Gainacre for $200,000 shortly after the merger, realizing a $75,000 gain.

Prior to the 1987 Act, unless Section 269 or 382 applied, L could apply its preacquisition losses to shelter any gains recognized on the disposition of the assets acquired from T. Thus, L could use its net operating loss carryforwards to offset the $75,000 gain on the sale of Gainacre. Because it was not clear that Section 269 would effectively deter this strategy, Congress became concerned that loss corporations would become vehicles for "laundering" the built-in gains of profitable target companies. Section 384—yet another attack on the real and perceived abuses flowing from corporate acquisitions—is the legislative response. Its purpose is to preclude a corporation from using its preacquisition losses to shelter built-in gains of another (usually, a target) corporation which are recognized within five years of an acquisition of the gain corporation's assets or stock. In the example above, L would be prevented from using its preacquisition net operating loss as a deduction against the $75,000 "recognized built-in gain" on the disposition of Gainacre.

Section 384 is triggered in two situations: (1) stock acquisitions, where one corporation acquires "control" (defined by reference to the 80 percent benchmark in Section 1504(a)(2)) of another corporation, and

(2) asset acquisitions in an acquisitive Type A, C or D reorganization, if either corporation is a "gain corporation"—i.e., a corporation having built-in gains.[1] As originally enacted in the 1987 Act, Section 384 applied only when a loss corporation acquired the stock or assets of a gain corporation, but TAMRA expanded the provision to apply regardless of which corporation acquired the other. If applicable, Section 384(a) provides that the corporation's income, to the extent attributable to "recognized built-in gains," shall not be offset by any "preacquisition loss" other than a preacquisition loss of the gain corporation. This punishment occurs during any "recognition period taxable year," which is any taxable year within the five-year period beginning on the "acquisition date."[2] Significantly, these rules apply whether or not there is a change in ownership in the stock of either corporation.

Understanding the operation of Section 384 requires a mastery of its glossary, much of which is borrowed from Section 382. The essential terms are as follows:

(1) The "acquisition date" is the date on which control is acquired, in the case of a stock acquisition, or the date of the transfer, in the case of an asset acquisition.[3]

(2) A "preacquisition loss" is as any net operating loss carryforward to the taxable year in which the acquisition date occurs and the portion of any net operating loss for the taxable year of the acquisition to the extent the loss is allocable to the period before the acquisition date.[4]

---

1. I.R.C. § 384(a), (c)(4) and (5). Section 384 does not displace any of the other Code provisions limiting loss carryovers—e.g., Sections 269, 382, and certain provisions in the consolidated return regulations. Congress has indicated that the limitations of Section 384 apply independently of and in addition to the limitations of Section 382. Staff of the Joint Committee on Taxation, Description of the Technical Corrections Bill of 1988, 100th Cong., 2d Sess. 421 (1988). Note that, in contrast to Section 269, the application of Section 384 is not dependent on the subjective intent of the acquiring corporation.

2. See I.R.C. §§ 384(c)(8); 382(h)(7). As amended by TAMRA, the Section 384 limitation applies to any "successor" corporation to the same extent it applied to its predecessor. I.R.C. § 384(c)(7). For example, assume that Loss Corporation ("L") acquires control of Gain Corporation ("G"), and the two corporations subsequently file a consolidated return. Income attributable to G's recognized built-in gains may not be offset by L's preacquisition losses during the subsequent five-year recognition period. If G is liquidated into L under Section 332 within five years of the acquisition, income attributable to G's recognized built-in gains may not be offset by L's preacquisition losses during the remainder of the five-year period. The same result would occur if L merged into G. See Staff of Joint Committee on Taxation, Description of the Technical Corrections Bill of 1988, 100th Cong., 2d Sess. 421 (1988).

3. I.R.C. § 384(c)(2).

4. I.R.C. § 384(c)(3)(A). In the case of a corporation with a net unrealized built-in loss, as defined by Section 382(h)(1)(B), the term "preacquisition loss" also includes any built-in loss recognized during the five-year recognition period. I.R.C. § 384(c)(3)(B).

(3) A "recognized built-in gain" is any gain recognized on the disposition of any asset during the five-year recognition period except to the extent that the gain corporation (in the case of an acquisition of control) or the acquiring corporation (in the case of an asset acquisition) establishes that the asset was not held by the gain corporation on the acquisition date, or that the gain accrued after the acquisition date.[5] Income items recognized after the acquisition date but attributable to prior periods are also treated as recognized built-in gain.[6] This definition should be familiar; it is similar to the definition of the same term in Section 382(h)(2)(A) except that the burden of proof is different. Under Section 382, the burden was on the taxpayer to establish that a built-in gain that was not exceeded by the recognized gain on disposition of an asset. Under Section 384, it is presumed that a gain recognized during the recognition period is a built-in gain unless the corporation establishes that the asset was not held on the acquisition date or that the recognized gain exceeds the built-in gain at the time of the acquisition.

(4) The amount of recognized built-in gain for any taxable year is limited to the "net unrealized built-in gain" reduced by recognized built-in gains for prior years in the recognition period which, but for Section 384, would have been offset by preacquisition losses.[7] For this purpose, the definition of "net unrealized built-in gain" is borrowed from Section 382(h)(3), substituting the acquisition date for the ownership "change date."[8] Thus, it is the excess of the aggregate fair market value of the assets of the "gain corporation" over the aggregate adjusted bases of those assets, except that the net unrealized built-in gain will be deemed to be zero unless it is greater than 25 percent of the fair market value of the corporation's assets other than cash and certain marketable securities.[9]

The limitations in Section 384(a) do not apply to the preacquisition loss of any corporation if such corporation and the gain corporation were members of the same "controlled group" at all times during the five-year period ending on the acquisition date. For this purpose, the definition of controlled group is borrowed from Section 1563 (as modified to generally require 50 percent common ownership of both voting power and value).[10]

5. I.R.C. § 384(c)(1)(A).
6. I.R.C. § 384(c)(1)(B).
7. I.R.C. § 384(c)(1)(C).
8. I.R.C. § 384(c)(4).
9. Id.
10. I.R.C. § 384(b). The common control testing period would be shortened if the gain corporation was not in existence for the full five year pre-acquisition date period by substituting its period of existence. I.R.C. § 384(b)(3).

As if the foregoing rules were not enough, Section 384(f) authorizes the Treasury to promulgate regulations as may be necessary to carry out the anti-abuse mission of the section.

PROBLEM

Gain Corp., which is wholly owned by individual A, has the following assets and no liabilities:

Asset	Adj. Basis	F.M.V.
Inventory	$150,000	$300,000
Machinery	300,000	200,000
Gainacre	100,000	350,000

Loss Corp., which is wholly owned by unrelated individual B, has $500,000 in net operating loss carryforwards.

Unless otherwise indicated below, assume that Loss Corp. acquired all the assets of Gain Corp. in a tax-free Type A reorganization on January 1, 1989. After the acquisition, B owned 80% and A owned 20% of the Loss Corp. stock. To what extent, if any, may Loss Corp. use its preacquisition net operating loss carryforwards against the gains recognized in the following alternative transactions:

(a) Loss Corp. sells Gainacre for $500,000 in 1990.

(b) Same as (a), above, except that Loss Corp. acquired all of Gain Corp.'s stock from A for cash (not making a § 338 election) on January 1, 1989, after which it liquidated Gain Corp. under § 332.

(c) Same as (a), above, except Loss Corp. also sells the inventory for $400,000 in 1990.

(d) Instead of (a)–(c), above, Loss Corp. sells Gainacre for $900,000 in 1995.

(e) Same as (a), above, except that Loss Corp. has no net operating loss carryforwards at the time of the acquisition but its only asset is Lossacre, which had a fair market value of $300,000 and an adjusted basis of $500,000. In 1990, Loss Corp. sells Lossacre for $200,000 at the same time that it sells Gainacre for $500,000.

CHAPTER 15. THE FUTURE OF SUBCHAPTER C

Page 701:

After the third full paragraph, add:

E. LEVERAGED BUYOUTS: THE PROBLEM OF EXCESSIVE DEBT

The incentive to capitalize a C corporation with debt and the difficulties in distinguishing between debt and equity were discussed in Chapter 4 of the main volume. The wave of corporate restructuring in the 1980's has raised the stakes on this issue. From 1984 to 1987, a variety of corporate transactions resulted in a reduction of $313.3 billion in corporate equity while new net corporate borrowing increased by $613.3 billion. A particular culprit, in the eyes of some observers, is a debt-financed form of acquisition known as the "leveraged buyout."

In early 1989, the Congressional tax-writing committees held hearings to examine the federal income tax aspects of corporate financial structures and to consider the problem of excessive debt and the possible options to eliminate or reduce the distinction between debt and equity. The background of the problem, some illustrative transactions, the policy issues and possible options are discussed in the excerpts below from a study prepared by the Joint Committee on Taxation in connection with these hearings.

EXCERPT FROM JOINT COMMITTEE ON TAXATION, FEDERAL INCOME TAX ASPECTS OF CORPORATE FINANCIAL STRUCTURES *

101st Cong., 1st Sess. (JCS 1–89, Jan. 18, 1989).

I. BACKGROUND

The United States is still in the midst of a period of rapid merger activity which began several years ago.[2] As this boom in merger activity has accelerated, correspondingly major, though less well publicized, changes in the role of debt, equity and corporate distributions have occurred which has resulted in an increasing use of debt by the corporate sector. The shift away from equity toward debt finance is not

---

* Some footnotes omitted.

2. Although "merger" is a term of art under the Internal Revenue Code, it generally will be used in this section of the pamphlet in the nontechnical sense to refer to an acquisition or takeover of one corporation by another corporation or group of investors.

solely due to leveraged buyouts nor is it a product of short-term trading of securities by market participants. Since the tax treatment of corporate debt has not changed recently, there is little evidence that the tax bias of debt over equity has led to increased takeover activity or changes in corporate financial structure. Many factors other than taxes affect financing activities and acquisitions. There are indications, however, that the tax system influences corporate merger and financing decisions and may serve as an additional incentive for debt finance.

The parallel shifts in corporate financing and merger activity have created concern for those with interests in monetary policy, the regulation of financial institutions and security markets, and antitrust and competitive policy, as well as tax policy. Some argue that the time and expense involved in corporate acquisitions divert resources and managerial energy from productive investment toward short-term goals; others claim this acquisition activity serves to redeploy corporate assets in a more efficient pattern and focuses management attention on the long-term goals of production and profitability. The changes in financing behavior cause some people to conclude that the U.S. economic system may now be more vulnerable to economic downturns and that the risk to private investors, the U.S. government, and the nation as a whole has increased. While the tax system may not be the cause for the recent changes in merger and corporate financial behavior, because the tax system does influence these decisions, it is important to identify the public policy goals that should determine the Federal government's response and the role that tax policy plays in achieving these goals. In addition, since over $94 billion in tax revenue was raised by the corporate income tax in fiscal year 1988, trends which reduce the corporate income tax base require careful scrutiny.

A. Corporate Restructurings that Affect Debt and Equity

There are a variety of transactions that affect the level of debt and equity in the corporate sector. Many of these transactions involve mergers and acquisitions, others do not; they all share the common trait that they may serve to reduce equity or increase debt in the corporate sector. What follows is a brief description of a few transactions and financing methods that may be of particular interest from a tax policy perspective.

Acquisitions.—Acquisitions for which the target shareholders receive cash in exchange for their shares, and in which the funding for the acquisition is provided by new debt issues or retained earnings of the acquiror, serve to reduce the level of corporate equity and generally to increase the level of debt relative to equity in the corporate sector. The acquisition process may take many forms, hostile or friendly, and may be relatively simple or involve any of the more complex maneuverings that have generated so much publicity.

Leveraged buyouts.—Leveraged buyouts are a particular form of debt-financed acquisition in which the acquiring group finances the acquisition of an existing target corporation, or a division or subsidiary of an existing company, primarily with debt secured by the assets or stock of the target corporation. Such an acquisition often produces unusually high debt to equity ratios (sometimes greater than ten to one) in the resulting company. The management of the target corporation frequently obtains a significant portion of the equity in the resulting company. The acquired corporation sometimes is taken private and, therefore, is no longer subject to the reporting requirements that apply to public corporations. It is common, however, sometimes after major asset sales or restructurings by the leveraged company, for the private company eventually to go public again, sometimes with a new infusion of equity.

Leveraged ESOPs.—An employee stock ownership plan (ESOP) is a type of tax-qualified pension plan that is designed to invest primarily in the securities of the employer maintaining the plan and that can be used as a technique of corporate finance. An ESOP that borrows to acquire employer securities is referred to as a leveraged ESOP. ESOPs may be used to effect a takeover and to defend against a hostile takeover. The Code contains numerous tax incentives designed to encourage the use and establishment of ESOPs and to facilitate the acquisition of employer securities by ESOPs through leveraging. Because of these tax benefits, use of an ESOP can result in a lower cost of borrowing than would be the case if traditional debt or equity financing were used. Despite the tax advantages, ESOPs may not be attractive in all cases because the rules relating to leveraged ESOPs require that some transfer of ownership to employees occur and may place limitations on the terms of the leveraging transaction. To the extent that ESOPs make leveraging more attractive, they may increase the degree of leverage in the economy.

Debt-for-equity swaps.—A corporation may exchange new debt for existing equity in the company. This transaction increases the degree of leverage of the corporation.

Redemptions of stock.—It has become increasingly common, particularly for large public corporations, to buy back their own shares. These repurchases of shares by the corporation will reduce outstanding equity and, particularly if financed by issues of debt, increase leverage.

Extraordinary distributions.—The quarterly or annual dividend has long been the prototypical method for distributing corporate earnings to equity investors. Sometimes a distribution amounting to a very large percentage of the value of the firm will be made to shareholders. This extraordinary distribution may be financed by debt and often is used in defensive restructurings in an attempt to avoid a takeover. The resulting corporate financial structure may be highly leveraged.

* * *

III. EXAMPLES OF TRANSACTIONS THAT INCREASE DEBT OR REDUCE EQUITY, AND TAX CONSEQUENCES

There are various transactions which can increase the debt of a corporation or reduce its equity. The discussion below describes broad categories of these transactions and uses examples to illustrate their tax consequences. The examples assume that no restrictions on interest deductions or other tax benefits stemming from interest expenses apply. In many cases, however, such limitations are applicable. For example, a taxpayer that pays foreign taxes in excess of the relevant foreign tax credit limitation (i.e., a taxpayer with excess foreign tax credits) will generally experience a net tax reduction of *less* than 34 cents on every dollar of additional interest expense; even though the interest is fully deductible, the foreign tax credit rules will apportion a fraction of each additional dollar of interest expense to foreign source gross income, further reducing the taxpayer's foreign tax credit limitation and hence its currently usable amount of foreign tax credits.

Although there are significant tax reasons which may lead a corporation to engage in these transactions, such transactions may also be motivated by reasons apart from Federal income tax considerations. For example, such transactions may be undertaken to increase the value of a corporation's stock, to enhance earnings per share calculations, to concentrate common stock holdings, to create treasury stock, as a defensive maneuver to ward off a takeover, or for other reasons.

* * *

B. Stock Repurchases

Description

A stock repurchase refers to a corporation redeeming (or buying back) its own shares from stockholders. A corporation may make a tender offer for a certain percentage of its shares at an announced price or a corporation may simply purchase its shares on the market. A corporation may fund a stock repurchase out of cash the corporation has on hand or it may borrow the funds.[67]

67. As an alternative to borrowing funds from an outside lender and using the proceeds to repurchase the stock of shareholders, a corporation may repurchase stock by issuing debt directly to redeeming shareholders. This is sometimes called a "debt-for-equity swap."

Tax consequences

A stock repurchase, whether financed out of cash the corporation has on hand or by borrowing, is generally a taxable transaction with respect to the redeeming shareholders. Taxable shareholders having their stock redeemed recognize any gain (i.e., the excess of the amount received over basis) or loss on the redemption of their shares.[68] There are no immediate tax consequences of a stock repurchase to the redeeming corporation.

A stock repurchase has further tax consequences to the redeeming corporation and to investors in the redeeming corporation over time. If a stock repurchase is financed with cash, the primary tax consequence is that the corporate assets of the redeeming corporation have been reduced. Corporate assets paid out to redeem shareholders' stock no longer produce earnings which are subject to the corporate income tax.[69] If the stock repurchase is financed through borrowing, the effect of the transaction is to replace the equity of the corporation with debt. Earnings of the corporation once available to be paid to shareholders as non-deductible dividends are instead paid to debtholders as deductible interest.[70] Thus, a stock redemption using borrowed funds enables the redeeming corporation to reduce its taxable income, or perhaps eliminate (or even generate current tax losses which it could carry back to obtain tax refunds).[71]

As indicated by the following example, the resulting reduction in Federal income taxes pays for increased returns to investors. To the extent increased investor returns are paid to taxable shareholders or debtholders, there may be an increase in investor-level taxes paid.

Example III–B

Consider the same facts as in Example III–A above, except that Company M announces it will repurchase up to $11 million of its shares at a redemption price of $120 per share, 50 percent more than the price at which the stock has been trading on the market. Taxable redeeming shareholders recognize gain or loss on the redemption of their shares.

---

68. Of course, there will be no tax imposed on those shareholders that are not subject to U.S. income tax on this income, i.e., certain foreign investors and tax-exempt investors such as pension funds.

69. As discussed in Part III.A. of this pamphlet, supra, this is also the result when the earnings of the distributing corporation are distributed to noncorporate shareholders in circumstances other than in connection with a stock repurchase.

70. A leveraged stock repurchase has exactly the same tax consequences as a leveraged distribution made by a corporation with respect to its stock.

71. A reduction in the redeeming corporation's Federal income tax liability could also increase its cash flow significantly. That increased cash flow might be sufficient to enable the redeeming corporation to cover most of its debt service obligations with respect to the borrowed funds and retire much of the debt over a period of years (although the redeeming company might also have to sell some of its assets to raise cash to assist it in paying off the loan).

At $120 per share, $11 million will purchase approximately 93 percent of Company M's outstanding shares. To finance the share repurchase, Company M issues bonds for $11 million paying 12 percent interest. Approximately 93 percent of Company M's outstanding shares are redeemed.

The distribution of the operating income of Company M before and after the stock repurchase is as follows:

	Before	After
Redeeming shareholders	$ 920,700	0
Bondholders	0	$1,320,000
Continuing shareholders	69,300	118,800
Corporate income taxes	510,000	61,200
Total operating income	1,500,000	1,500,000
Earnings per share	10	16.20

The leveraged stock redemption has redistributed the income stream of Company M in the same way that the leveraged distribution with respect to stock redistributed the income stream, except that the continuing shareholders of Company M, rather than all the shareholders of Company M, receive the profit of $118,800. The redeeming shareholders of Company M who used to get $920,700 a year in dividends before the redemption receive no part of the income stream after the redemption. New bondholders receive interest of 12 percent a year on $11 million, or $1.32 million. This is one-third more than the entire amount of Company M's after-tax income before the stock repurchases even though the operating income of Company M is unchanged. Continuing shareholders of Company M receive the profit of $118,800 (the remainder of Company M's income after taxes and interest expense).

The taxable income of Company M has been reduced from $1.5 million to $180,000 ($1.5 million minus $1.32 million) because most of the earnings of Company M are now paid out as deductible interest payments. The resulting reduction of corporate Federal income taxes from $510,000 to $61,200 exactly pays for the increased returns to the new bondholders and the continuing shareholders. Depending on whether the increased returns are paid to taxable bondholders and shareholders, there may be an increase in investor-level Federal income taxes paid.

Note also that the earnings per share of Company M have gone up from $10 per share ($990,000 divided by 99,000 shares outstanding) before the leveraged buyout to $16.20 per share ($118,800 divided by 7,333 shares outstanding) after the leveraged buyout. If the stock will still sell for 8 times its earnings on the market after the leveraged buyout, the stock price would rise from $80 to $129.60 ($16.20 times 8).

Taxpayers have also sought similar tax results in connection with so-called "unbundled stock units." On December 5, 1988, four publicly traded companies—American Express Co., Dow Chemical Co., Pfizer Inc. and Sara Lee Corp.—announced offers to their shareholders to exchange a certain portion of their outstanding common stock for unbundled stock units comprised of three separate securities:

(1) a 30–year deep-discount bond which will pay quarterly interest in an amount equal to the current dividend of the common stock exchanged;

(2) a share of preferred stock which will yield dividends equal to any increase in the dividend yield of the company's common stock; and

(3) an "equity appreciation certificate" which entitles the holder to acquire one share of common stock for an amount equal to the redemption value of the 30–year bond plus a share of the preferred stock. The new bond in effect would convert what had been nondeductible ordinary dividends into deductible interest payments, in addition to providing corporate deductions for an element of original issue discount.[72]

Actual transactions

Stock repurchases have become common corporate transactions. A list of the largest stock repurchases during 1988 published by *The Wall Street Journal* indicated that the largest 21 stock buy-back announcements of 1988 were intended to retire almost 500 million shares of stock worth approximately $23.8 billion. Ten transactions were listed with a value in excess of $1 billion. The largest transactions listed were the following: (1) UAL Corporation buying back 35.5 million common shares with a value of $2.84 billion; (2) International Business Machines Corporation buying back 17.8 million common shares with a value of $2 billion; (3) CSX Corp. buying back 60 million shares with a value of $1.86 billion; and (4) Sears Roebuck buying back 40 million common shares with a value of $1.75 billion.

C. Acquisitions Including Leveraged Buyouts

The acquisition of one corporation by another corporation may be structured in many different ways. An acquiring corporation may

---

72. The four companies currently plan to replace between 6.5 and 20 percent of their outstanding common stock with unbundled stock units. It has been estimated that the four corporations issuing unbundled stock units could save, in the aggregate, up to $5.9 billion in Federal income taxes over the 20–year life of the bonds. Aggregate tax savings in the first year after the exchange may be as much as $85 million, with annual tax savings steadily rising through the 30–year bond term. *New York Times*, December 7, 1988, p. D1. The Internal Revenue Service has not ruled on the tax treatment of unbundled stock units.

acquire control of the "target" corporation or it may acquire a small interest in the stock of another corporation as an investment. The acquiring corporation may finance the acquisition with debt (either by a new borrowing of the necessary funds or by keeping an old borrowing outstanding), or with its own retained earnings, or with funds contributed as new equity capital by investors.

An acquisition of the control of a target company may be a hostile or friendly transaction. It may be structured as an acquisition of the stock of the target company or an acquisition of the assets of the target company. The target company may continue to operate as an independent company in the same manner as before it was acquired, or it may be absorbed into the acquiring company or other companies owned by the acquiring company, or it may cease operations entirely and its assets be divided and sold.

1. Stock acquisitions out of retained earnings

A corporation may finance the acquisition of the stock of another corporation with internally generated funds (i.e., its retained earnings). The purchase of the stock has no tax consequences to the shareholders of the purchasing corporation. Likewise, there are no tax consequences to the acquired corporation as a result of the acquisition. The taxable shareholders of the acquired corporation recognize any gain or loss on the sale of their shares.

There are generally no immediate tax consequences to the purchasing corporation as a result of the transaction. However, the total amount of funds in corporate solution, the earnings of which are subject to a corporate-level tax, may be reduced by the amount spent for the acquisition to the extent that shares are acquired by the acquiring corporation from noncorporate shareholders. Moreover, no compensating additional corporate tax may arise when earnings of the acquired corporation are distributed to the acquiring corporation. This is because earnings of the target company which are distributed to the acquiring corporation as dividends will either be nontaxable under the consolidated return rules, or, if the corporations do not file a consolidated return, will be eligible for the dividends received deduction.

2. Debt-financed stock acquisitions including leveraged buyouts

A corporation may finance the acquisition of another corporation's stock by borrowing. The acquiring corporation may borrow using its own assets as security for the loan or it may borrow using the assets of the target company as security for the loan. In either case, debt has been substituted for equity at the corporate level. When the debt is secured by the acquired corporation's assets, the transaction is more likely to be called a "leveraged buyout."

Description

A leveraged buyout refers to a particular type of debt-financed acquisition of a "target" corporation.[74] The purchasers borrow most of the purchase price of the target company, using the assets of the target company as security for the loan. After the acquisition, the target corporation may be able to service the debt obligation out of its cash flow from operations or the purchaser may sell the assets of the target company and use the proceeds to retire the debt.

A leveraged buyout may occur in many different contexts and may be used by many different types of purchasers. The leveraged buyout, also sometimes called a bootstrap acquisition, has long been used to acquire private (i.e., closely held) corporations. More recently, leveraged buyouts have been used to acquire large public companies. A public company may be "taken private" through a leveraged buyout if the purchasers of the target public corporation are a relatively small group of investors. If the purchasers of the target corporation in a leveraged buyout include the current management of the target company, the transaction is sometimes called a "management buyout." A division or a subsidiary of a company also may be purchased through a leveraged buyout.

A leveraged buyout of a target company is usually accomplished by a debt-financed tender offer by the existing corporation for its outstanding publicly held stock, or, alternatively, by a tender offer for the target corporation's stock by a largely debt-financed shell corporation established for this purpose. The target corporation will repurchase its stock from its shareholders or the shell corporation will buy all the stock of the target corporation.[76] If a shell corporation is used, the target corporation and the shell corporation will typically merge immediately after the acquisition.

As mentioned above, most of the funds for a leveraged buyout transaction are borrowed, with the purchasers contributing only a small amount of their own funds as equity. Lenders for these transactions have been banks, investment banks, insurance companies, pension funds, and pools of investors. Debt terms reflect the degree of leverage and the loan security involved. Some of the debt incurred frequently is below investment grade, i.e., so-called "junk" bonds.

74. In what is called a "reverse leveraged buyout," public companies which had been converted to private companies in a leveraged buyout become public companies again, with their shares being sold in a public offering to shareholders.

76. Shareholders of the target company typically receive a premium for their stock above the price at which the stock has been trading on the market.

Tax consequences

A leveraged buyout is generally a taxable transaction with respect to the shareholders of the target corporation.[77] Taxable shareholders selling their stock recognize gain or loss on the sale of their shares.[78] There are no immediate tax consequences of a leveraged buyout at the corporate level since generally neither the repurchase by the target corporation of its own shares nor the purchase of the target corporation's shares by a shell corporation followed by the merger of the target and shell corporation is a taxable transaction.

The primary tax consequences of a leveraged buyout to the target corporation arise from the fact that the equity of the corporation has been replaced by debt. Income of the target corporation once paid to investors as nondeductible dividends on stock is instead paid to creditors as tax-deductible interest on debt.[79] As a result of the interest deductions generated by the borrowing in a leveraged buyout, the target corporation may have little, if any, taxable income in the years following a leveraged buyout and may claim loss carrybacks producing a refund of taxes paid prior to the acquisition.[80] Because the target corporation pays little, if any, of its operating income as Federal income taxes, the portion of the target corporation's income that was once being paid to the Federal government as Federal income taxes may instead be redirected to increase investor returns. However, to the extent increased investor returns are paid to taxable shareholders or holders of debt, there may be an increase in investor-level Federal income taxes paid.

Example III-C

Consider the same facts as in Example III-A. Rather than the management of Company M announcing a distribution with respect to its stock, Company M is acquired in a leveraged buyout. The acquirors pay $120 per share of stock, or 50 percent more than the price at which the stock has been trading on the market, for a total price of $11.88 million. Taxable selling shareholders recognize gain or loss on the sale of their shares.

The acquirors put up $880,000 of their own funds and raise the remaining $11 million of the purchase price by issuing notes paying 12

---

77. Of course, there will be no tax imposed on those shareholders that are not subject to U.S. income tax on their income, i.e., certain foreign investors and tax-exempt investors such as pension funds.

78. Taxable shareholders will generally recognize gain (i.e., the excess of the amount received over their basis in the stock) because acquirors typically pay a substantial premium for stock in a leveraged buyout transaction.

79. A leveraged buyout has exactly the same tax effect as a leveraged distribution made by a corporation with respect to its stock and a leveraged stock redemption.

80. Indeed, the target corporation may be able to service its debt obligations out of a cash flow and reduced (or reduced less) by taxes.

percent interest to be secured by the assets of Company M. The annual income of Company M after the leveraged buyout is unchanged.

The distribution of the operating income of Company M before and after the leveraged buyout is as follows:

	Before	After
Company M shareholders	$ 990,000	0
Bondholders	0	$1,320,000
Acquirors	0	118,800
Corporate income taxes	510,000	61,200
Total operating income	1,500,000	1,500,000

The leveraged buyout has redistributed the income stream of Company M in the same way that the leveraged distribution with respect to stock, and the leveraged stock redemption, redistributed the income stream of Company M. However, the acquirors of Company M, rather than all the shareholders (in the case of a distribution with respect to stock) or the continuing shareholders of Company M (in the case of a stock redemption) receive the profit of $118,800. Company M shareholders who before the transaction received $990,000 a year in dividends now receive no distributions. New bondholders receive interest of 12 percent on $11 million, or $1.32 million. This is one third more than the entire amount of Company M's after-tax income before the leveraged buyout, even though the operating income of Company M is the same before and after the leveraged buyout.

The taxable income of Company M has, however, been reduced from $1.5 million to $180,000 ($1.5 million minus $1.32 million) because most of the income of the company is paid out to investors as interest rather than dividends. Federal income taxes are thereby reduced from $510,000 to $61,200. Acquirors make an after-tax profit of $118,800 (pre-tax profit of $180,000 reduced by Federal income tax of $61,200), a 13.4 percent return on their $880,000 equity investment. The income tax reduction of $448,800 exactly pays for the increased returns to investors (bondholders and the acquirors) as a result of the leveraged buyout. Depending on whether the increased investor returns are paid to taxable shareholders or holders of debt, there may be an increase in investor-level Federal income taxes paid.

Actual transactions

Leveraged buyouts of public companies have greatly increased in recent years, and the amounts involved in such transactions have risen dramatically. (See the discussion in part I.B. of this pamphlet, supra.) The largest leveraged buyout transaction to date is the proposed acquisition of RJR Nabisco by the investment firm of Kohlberg Kravis Roberts & Co. ("KKR") for nearly $25 billion. It is expected that this acquisition will be completed by February 1989. Other large leveraged buyout transactions include the acquisition of Beatrice Companies by KKR for $6.25 billion in April 1986, and the management buyout of R.H. Macy & Co., Inc. for $3.5 billion in July 1986.

Newspaper reports indicate that out of the approximately $25 billion needed for the RJR Nabisco acquisition, more than $22.5 billion will be borrowed. Secured bank debt will account for approximately $17.5 billion of the borrowing, with most of the remainder being provided by investment banking firms. A pool of investors organized by KKR will put up $1.5 billion as an equity investment. It has been reported that KKR will contribute approximately $15 million of its own funds as equity. RJR Nabisco shareholders will be paid $109 for each share of common stock. This is almost twice the price at which the stock was trading immediately prior to the announcement of the possible sale of the company. It has been reported that due to increased interest deductions, RJR Nabisco could save up to $682 million annually in Federal and state income taxes and be able to seek the refund of additional amounts of taxes paid in prior years due to the carryback of net operating losses. Other reports have projected the annual savings at $370 million.

In the Beatrice transaction, each common shareholder received $50 per share ($40 in cash). This price of $50 per share was 45 percent higher than the market value of the stock one month prior to the announcement date of the first offer. Financing for the Beatrice leveraged buyout included $6.5 billion in debt and $1.35 billion in equity capital. Four billion dollars of the debt was lent by banks and $2.5 billion came from a new issue of high yield bonds. The equity came from two sources. Six hundred million came from a buyout fund organized by KKR and subscribed to by institutional investors and $750 million came from converting existing common stock to a new issue of preferred stock.

In the Macy transaction, each common share of stock outstanding received $68 in cash. This price of $68 per share was 55 percent higher than the market value of the stock one month prior to the announcement date of the first offer. On completion of the Macy leveraged buyout, the management group held 20 percent of the new company stock and an additional 20 percent was held by General Electric Co.'s credit union. Financing for the Macy leveraged buyout totalled approximately $3.7 billion. Out of this amount, almost $3.2 billion was debt: $770 million was lent from banks, $1.625 billion came from new issues of high yield bonds, and $800 million came from notes secured by mortgages. The remaining $500 million of the financing consisted of $200 million of excess cash of Macy's and $300 million was equity capital contributed by the acquirors.

IV. POLICY ISSUES

The recent wave of debt-financed mergers and acquisitions, both friendly and hostile, and the significant changes in patterns of corporate financing and distributions raise a number of public policy issues, including: (1) does the tax system encourage corporate debt financing relative to equity financing; (2) do leveraged buyouts increase economic efficiency or do they merely transfer wealth; (3) does the growth in corporate debt finance threaten macroeconomic stability; (4) does increasing leverage place additional demands on Federal guarantees of the financial system; and (5) does the role of ESOPs and tax-exempt institutions in these transactions reflect sound social policy?

A. Tax Advantage of Debt Versus Equity

The total effect of the tax system on the incentives for corporations to use debt or equity depends on the interaction between the tax treatment at the shareholder and corporate levels.

The case of no income taxes.—In a simple world without taxes or additional costs in times of financial distress, economic theory suggests that the value of a corporation, as measured by the total value of the outstanding debt and equity, would be unchanged by the degree of leverage of the firm. This conclusion explicitly recognizes that debt issued by the corporation represents an ownership right to future income of the corporation in a fashion similar to that of equity. In this simple world there would be no advantage to debt or to equity and the debt-equity ratio of the firm would not affect the cost of financing investment.

Effect of corporate income tax

Tax advantages

Taxes greatly complicate this analysis. Since the interest expense on debt is deductible for computing the corporate income tax while the return to equity is not, the tax at the corporate level provides a strong incentive for debt rather than equity finance.

The advantages of debt financing can be illustrated by comparing two corporations with $1,000 of assets that are identical except for financial structure: the first is entirely equity financed; while the second is 50-percent debt financed. Both corporations earn $150 of operating income. The all-equity corporation pays $51 in corporate tax and retains or distributes $99 of after-tax income ($150 less $51). Thus, as shown in Table IV-A, the return on equity is 9.9 percent ($99 divided by $1,000).

Table IV-A.—Effect of Debt Financing on Returns to Equity Investment

Item	All-equity corporation	50-percent debt-financed corporation
Beginning Balance Sheet:		
Total assets	$1,000	$1,000
Debt	0	500
Shareholders' equity	1,000	500
Income Statement:		
Operating income	150	150
Interest expense	0	50
Taxable income	150	100
Income tax	51	34
Income after corporate tax	99	66
Return on Equity [1] (percent)	9.9	13.2

[1] Return on equity is computed as income after corporate tax divided by beginning shareholders' equity.

The leveraged corporation is financed by $500 of debt and $500 of stock. If the interest rate is 10 percent, then interest expense is $50 (10 percent times $500). Taxable income is $100 after deducting interest expense. The leveraged corporation is liable for $34 in corporate tax (34 percent times $100) and distributes or retains $66 of after-tax income ($100 less $34). Consequently, the return on equity is 13.2 percent ($66 divided by $500). Thus, as shown in Table IV-A, increasing the debt ratio from zero to 50 percent increases the rate of return on equity from 9.9 to 13.2 percent.

This arithmetic demonstrates that a leveraged corporation can generate a higher return on equity (net of corporate income tax) than an unleveraged company or, equivalently, that an unleveraged company needs to earn a higher profit before corporate tax to provide investors the same return net of corporate tax as could be obtained with an unleveraged company. More generally, the return on equity rises with increasing debt capitalization so long as the interest rate is less than the pre-tax rate of return on corporate assets. This suggests that the Code creates an incentive to raise the debt-equity ratio to the point where the corporate income tax (or outstanding equity) is eliminated.

Costs of financial distress

With higher levels of debt the possibility of financial distress increases, as do the expected costs to the firm which occur with such distress. These additional costs include such items as the increase in the costs of debt funds; constraints on credit, expenditure or operating decisions; and the direct costs of being in bankruptcy. These expected costs of financial distress may, at sufficiently high debt-equity ratios, offset the corporate tax advantage to additional debt finance.

Effect of shareholder income tax

The above analysis focuses solely on the effect of interest deductibility at the corporate level. Shareholder-level income taxation may offset to some degree the corporate tax incentive for corporate debt relative to equity.

Shareholder treatment of debt and equity

The conclusion that debt is tax favored relative to equity remains unchanged if interest on corporate debt and returns on equity are taxed at the same effective rate to investors. In this case, the returns to investors on both debt and equity are reduced proportionately by the income tax; the advantage to debt presented by corporate tax deductibility remains. One noteworthy exception exists if the marginal investments on both debt and equity are effectively tax-exempt. Given the previously documented importance of tax-exempt pension funds in the bond and equity markets, this case may be of some importance.

Shareholder level tax treatment of equity

In general, returns to shareholders and debtholders are not taxed the same. Although dividends, like interest income, are taxed currently, equity income in other forms may reduce the effective investor-level tax on equity below that on debt. First, the firm may retain earnings and not pay dividends currently. In general, the accumulation of earnings by the firm will cause the value of the firm's shares to rise. Rather than being taxed currently on corporate earnings, a shareholder will be able to defer the taxation on the value of the retained earnings reflected in the price of the stock until the shareholder sells the stock. Thus, even though the tax rates on interest, dividends, and capital gains are the same, the ability to defer the tax on returns from equity reduces the effective rate of individual tax on equity investment below that on income from interest on corporate debt.

Other aspects of capital gain taxation serve to reduce further the individual income tax on equity. Since tax on capital gain is normally triggered after a voluntary recognition event (e.g., the sale of stock), the taxpayer can time the realization of capital gain income when the effective rate of tax is low. The rate of tax could be low if the taxpayer is in a low or zero tax bracket because other income is abnormally low, if other capital losses shelter the capital gain, or if changes in the tax law cause the statutory rate on capital gains to be low. Perhaps most important, the step up in the adjusted tax basis of the stock upon the death of the shareholder may permit the shareholder's heirs to avoid tax completely on capital gains. For all these reasons, the effective rate of tax on undistributed earnings may be already quite low.

Corporations can distribute their earnings to owners of equity in forms that generally result in less tax to shareholders than do dividend distributions. Share repurchases have become an important method of distributing corporate earnings to equity holders. When employed by large publicly traded firms, repurchases of the corporation's own shares permit the shareholders to treat the distribution as a sale of stock (i.e., to obtain capital gain treatment, and recover the basis in the stock without tax). The remaining shareholders may benefit because they have rights to a larger fraction of the firm and may see a corresponding increase in the value of their shares. Thus, less individual tax will generally be imposed on a $100 repurchase of stock than on $100 of dividends. In addition, share repurchases allow shareholders to choose whether to receive corporate distributions by choosing whether to sell or retain shares, so as to minimize tax liability.[94]

Acquisitions of the stock of one corporation for cash or property of another corporation provides a similar method for distributing corporate earnings out of corporate solution with less shareholder tax than through a dividend. The target shareholders generally treat the acquisition as a sale and recover their basis free of tax. For purposes of analyzing the individual tax effect of corporate earnings disbursements, this transaction can be thought of as equivalent to a stock merger of the target with the acquiror followed by the repurchase of the target shareholders' shares by the resulting merged firm. The result is similar to the case of a share repurchase in that cash is distributed to shareholders with less than the full dividend tax, except that two firms are involved instead of one.

Since dividends typically are subject to more tax than other methods for providing returns to shareholders, the puzzle of why firms pay dividends remains. Because dividends are paid at the discretion of the firm, it appears that firms cause their shareholders to pay more tax on equity income than is strictly necessary.[95] Until a better understanding of corporate distribution policy exists, the role of dividend taxation on equity financing decisions remain uncertain.

To summarize, although the current taxation of dividends to investors is clearly significant, there are numerous reasons why the overall individual tax on equity investments may be less than that on interest income from debt. Since the effective shareholder tax on returns from

---

94. Some have proposed that the taxation of share repurchases follow the taxation of dividend distributions at the investor level. One method by which this could be done is to treat the repurchase as a pro rata dividend to all shareholders followed by a pro rata sale of shares of the selling shareholders to the remaining shareholders. See, Chirelstein, "Optional Redemptions and Optional Dividends: Taxing the Repurchase of Common Shares," 78 Yale Law Journal 739 (1969).

95. The trends outlined in Part I.A demonstrate that corporations are shifting away from dividends as the predominant method for distributing income.

equity may be less than that on debt holdings, the shareholder tax may offset some or all of the advantage to debt at the corporate level.

Interaction of corporate and shareholder taxation

With shareholders in different income tax brackets, high tax rate taxpayers will tend to concentrate their wealth in the form of equity and low tax rate taxpayers will tend to concentrate their wealth in the form of debt. The distribution of wealth among investors with different marginal tax rates affects the demand for investments in the form of debt or equity. The interaction between the demand of investors, and the supply provided by corporations, determines the aggregate amount of corporate debt and equity in the economy.

At some aggregate mix between debt and equity, the difference in the investor-level tax on income from equity and debt may be sufficient to offset completely, at the margin, the apparent advantage of debt at the corporate level. Even if the difference in investor tax treatment of debt and equity is not sufficient to offset completely the corporate tax advantage, the advantage to debt may be less than the corporate-level tax treatment alone would provide.

Some believe that, because the top personal tax rate was reduced below the top corporate tax rate in the 1986 Act and because the share of wealth held by tax-exempt entities is substantial, the tax advantage of debt at the corporate level outweighs its disadvantages to investors.[96] They would argue that changes in tax law have provided the motive force in the drive toward higher leverage. However, given that the observed changes in corporate financial behavior began well before 1986, the changes due to the 1986 Act may be of relatively little importance in determining changes in leverage and acquisition behavior. The individual rate reductions in the Economic Recovery Tax Act of 1981, some respond, started the shift toward more debt in corporate structures and the 1986 Act merely provided another push in that direction.

Implications for policy

The analysis above suggests that any policy change designed to reduce the tax incentive for debt must consider the interaction of both corporate and shareholder taxes. For example, proposals to change the income tax rates for individuals or corporations will change the incentive for corporate debt. Likewise, proposals to change the tax treat-

---

[96]. Merton Miller, "The Modigliani–Miller Propositions After Thirty Years," Journal of Economic Perspectives, Fall 1988, pp. 99–120. Also see the discussion of corporate integration in part V.A.1 of this pamphlet, infra, for a numerical analysis of various possible total tax effects and the effect of the Tax Reform Act of 1986.

ment of tax-exempt entities may alter the aggregate mix and distribution of debt and equity.

In addition, proposals to reduce the bias toward debt over equity, for example, by reducing the total tax on dividends, must confront the somewhat voluntary nature of the dividend tax. Since the payment of dividends by corporations generally is discretionary and other means exist for providing value to shareholders with less tax, corporations can affect the level of shareholder level tax incurred. Until a better understanding of the determinants of corporate distribution behavior exists, the total impact of policies designed to reduce the bias between debt and equity are uncertain.

* * *

V. POSSIBLE OPTIONS AND RELATED POLICY CONSIDERATIONS

A. Eliminate or Reduce the Distinction Between Debt and Equity by Integrating the Corporate and Individual Income Tax Systems

[Integration of the corporate and individual income taxes is discussed in the excerpt at pages 687–695 of the main text. Ed.]

* * *

B. Eliminate or Reduce the Distinction Between Debt and Equity by Limiting Interest Deductions

Interest disallowance proposals should be evaluated with reference to various policy issues. These issues include: the potential erosion of the business tax base (including but not necessarily limited to the corporate tax base); the proper measurement of economic income; the non-tax economic impact of business leverage; and whether certain specified types of transactions should be discouraged for various other non-tax economic reasons. In addition, administrability and fairness issues may be raised.

Particular interest disallowance proposals may address one or more of these issues. The proposals may be more or less comprehensive in treatment of the issues they do address. Because the proposals differ widely in the nature of the issues they address, it is necessary to determine which policy issues are considered significant in order to evaluate the desirability of any particular proposal.

The following discussion first describes a number of interest disallowance proposals and discusses the principal issues they address. The discussion then describes certain additional issues common to many of the proposals.

1. Broad interest disallowance proposals not dependent on particular types of corporate transactions

All interest deductions above a specified amount could be disallowed. There are several variations of this approach, each of which computes the amount of the disallowance based on different factors. The factors selected indicate the policy objectives of the proposals.

a. *Disallow a flat percentage of all interest deductions*

Under this approach, the amount of nondeductible interest would be a percentage of total interest expense. This approach principally addresses concerns about erosion of the revenue base and about the role of debt in facilitating tax arbitrage. It does not address issues of the proper measurement of income (either by trying to distinguish debt from equity, or by trying to limit interest deductions where the debt supports activities that do not produce income taxable to the entity incurring the debt). It also is not limited to any particular types of transactions that might be considered undesirable for non-tax reasons.

While revenue concerns are the main basis for this particular approach, issues arise regarding its effectiveness. For example, if the deduction denial is related only to a percentage of total interest expense, it might be possible for taxpayers in some circumstances to increase the stated interest amount beyond the amount they might have stated absent this provision, thus continuing to reap the benefit of the deduction. Present law provides certain bright-line rules designed to prevent the interest component of an obligation from being understated; but it has no comparable rules designed to prevent the overstatement of interest. Issues related to the design of such rules are addressed below in connection with other proposals.

The impact of this proposal will vary dramatically from industry to industry. For example, financial intermediaries, such as banks, may see enormous increases in taxable income, even though their loans may bear low interest rates. Likewise, this proposal will disproportionately affect activities which support high degrees of leverage, such as real estate, even though the debt involved may not be particularly risky.

b. *Disallow interest deductions in excess of a specified rate of return to investors*

This approach would disallow interest deductions in excess of a specified rate of return to investors. Deductions not in excess of that rate still would be permitted. The rate could be determined by reference to a rate deemed to represent that of a relatively risk-free investment (for example, the rate on comparable-term Treasury obligations issued at the time of the borrowing, or a few points above that rate). The rate could fluctuate as the reference rate fluctuates.

As with the approach described above, this approach addresses concerns about erosion of the tax base, but to the extent the rate selected reflects a measurement of "risk," this approach also might be described as an attempt to properly measure economic income. If one accepts the premise that all interest on debt is properly deductible without regard to whether the debt supports an asset that produces taxable income, and the further premise that the most fundamental basis for distinguishing debt from equity is the degree of investor risk, this approach seeks to deny a deduction for the "risk" element of stated interest on the theory it more nearly resembles a dividend distribution, while continuing to permit the non-risk portion to be fully deductible.

A primary issue with respect to this type of approach is the selection of the permitted deductible interest rate. To the extent the rate is selected in an attempt to identify excessive risk, questions may be raised regarding the accuracy of a risk analysis based solely on interest rate. On the other hand, to the extent the proposal is viewed as one of administrative convenience designed to address revenue concerns and avoid the need to distinguish between debt and equity, the accuracy of any risk analysis may be considered less important.

Non-tax policy issues also may arise. For example, even though it is arguable that a high degree of risk suggests an equity investment, and that a high interest rate suggests a high degree of risk, the practical result of such an approach may be that certain start-up firms, or firms involved in inherently risky ventures, may be more restricted in their ability to deduct all of the interest demanded by investors than other more established or stable firms. Variations in the permitted rate might be adopted for such situations; however, arguments then may be raised that whichever taxpayers are permitted the higher deductions may obtain a competitive advantage over other ventures also involving risk, which may have implications for neutrality of the tax system in this respect.

c. *Disallow interest deductions based on inflation: interest indexing*

This approach would disallow a portion of interest deductions based on inflation. A corresponding portion of the recipient's interest income would be treated as nontaxable.

1984 Treasury proposal

The Treasury proposals in 1984 suggested a plan which generally would have rendered the same specified fraction of interest non-deductible and non-includable. Home mortgage interest and a de minimis amount of other individual interest were exempt from these provisions.

The Treasury proposal assumed a specified real pre-tax interest rate and would have calculated a percentage each year based on this assumed real rate relative to the sum of inflation and the assumed real interest rate. The allowable interest deduction (and inclusion) each year would have been calculated by multiplying nominal interest payments (and receipts) by this percentage, which would be published periodically by the tax authorities.

As a method for indexing debt, the proposal was relatively simple. Even so, it still had numerous difficulties. Because it applied a single fraction to all interest it did a poor job of coping with debt of differing risk characteristics; in particular, it made too large a percentage of interest on risky debt nondeductible and non-includable. Also, if the fraction were applied to financial intermediaries (e.g., banks), their income could be very lightly taxed. As pointed out by Treasury at the time, even with its problems, the method was likely to provide a more appropriate measure of income than the current method of deducting and including all nominal interest.

Other proposals

Other methods of indexing may better measure real interest deductions but at the cost of increased complexity. One proposal would require the restatement of interest paid by subtracting out the inflationary component of the interest rate. For example, if one paid $100 of interest at a 10 percent nominal rate and the rate of inflation were 7 percent, then one would calculate the inflationary component of the interest paid at a 7 percent rate ($70) and subtract that amount from the interest actually paid. The difference ($30) would be the allowed amount of deductible interest. Similar calculations would be necessary for purposes of income inclusion. This proposal, while having fewer distortions than the Treasury proposal, is significantly more complex and administratively difficult. In general, proposals designed to measure the appropriate amount of interest make a trade-off between simplicity and accuracy.

Issues generally applicable to indexing

A number of issues arise with respect to interest indexing. A principal concern is determining the amount of correction to interest expense or income that accurately reflects inflation. It may be necessary to determine a "real" interest rate prior to risk considerations. Even assuming a correct adjustment is identified, it may be necessary for administrative convenience to apply that adjustment in a relatively rough manner that does not fully account for different real interest rates over different periods of a year. It may be difficult to provide an administrable adjustment that does not involve windfalls to some taxpayers.

Indexing only interest but not other long-term arrangements may put additional pressure on the determination as to whether an instrument is properly characterized as debt. For example, depending on the relative tax situations of the parties, indexing only interest may make it more desirable for a taxpayer with a relatively high effective tax rate to hold an instrument characterized as debt rather than equity. Similarly, it may be more desirable for an arrangment to be characterized as a lending arrangement rather than a lease. To the extent parties in different tax situations recharacterized their arrangements to take advantage of tax arbitrage potential in this additional new disparity between the treatment of debt and other arrangements, there could be a corresponding revenue concern. On the other hand, it can be argued that failure to index may perpetuate a far greater revenue loss if the holders of debt instruments tend to be entities with a low effective tax rate and borrowers tend to be taxpayers with a higher effective rate who are obtaining an excessive interest deduction.

Exempting certain classes of debt, such as home mortgages, from indexing proposals may cause large tax-induced distortions of asset portfolios. Thus, excluding home mortgages would increase further the tax incentives for owner-occupied housing.

Any proposal that reduces interest inclusions and deductions to the same degree will generally reduce nominal interest rates. Because of the fall in nominal interest, the value of tax exemption to pension funds and other tax-exempt institutions will be less than it would be under a system without indexing.

d. Disallow interest deductions in excess of a specified percentage of taxable income (or earnings and profits) as computed before the deductions

This approach would limit the interest deduction by reference to taxable income (or alternatively, earnings and profits) determined prior to the deduction. For example, one version of this approach would limit the deduction to no more than 50 percent (or some other specified percentage) of the taxable income of the corporation computed without regard to the interest deduction. Such an approach was adopted in the 1986 Senate version of H.R. 3838 (the Tax Reform Act of 1986) but was limited to situations where the lender was related to the payor corporation by at least 50–percent ownership and was a tax-exempt or foreign entity that would not pay U.S. tax on interest received from the payor corporation (Senate amendment to H.R. 3838, sec. 984 (1986)). One variation would limit the deduction to no more than 50 percent (or some other specified percentage) of the earnings and profits or the corporation computed without regard to the deduction. Another variation would apply the limitation only for minimum tax purposes.

This approach is principally addressed to revenue concerns and attempts to provide a rough but practical alternative to complex rules for distinguishing equity from debt, which assures that interest alone does not shelter taxable income to an unacceptable degree.

The limitation to a specified percentage of taxable income (or earnings and profits) might arguably be viewed as reflecting concerns about proper measurement of income, on the theory that when interest deductions alone consume a significant proportion of otherwise taxable income, this may suggest excessive risk to the lender implying an equity interest. However, this particular approach is not a targeted method of identifying situations of risk. This is because the ability to pay back indebtedness depends largely on the capacity of the debtor to generate cash flow, either from current operations or from sales of appreciated assets. Neither taxable income nor earnings and profits is an adequate measure of such capacity. For example, an entity with significant cash flow potential may have low taxable income because of other tax deductions that do not reflect economic losses (for example, accelerated depreciation), or because assets are currently held for appreciation and not for current income. The use of earnings and profits as a limitation similarly does not take account of items such as unrealized appreciation, which may be sufficient to avoid undue risk to the debtholder.

This approach also raises an issue whether it is desirable to limit interest deductions, thus increasing the effective tax rate, in times of recession or when taxable income is otherwise small due to real economic losses.

[The report went on to discuss options under which corporate interest deductions would be disallowed in transactions that reduce the corporate equity base or in more specified acquisitions or stock purchase transactions—e.g., proposals introduced in Congress that would limit interest deductions in the case of certain corporate repurchase transactions involving identifiable "risk" or in certain debt-financed acquisitions where appreciation on corporate assets is untaxed, or in certain hostile takeover situations. Ed.]

* * *

C. Combination Interest Disallowance and Dividend Relief Options

1. Provide deductible rate of return for corporate-level equity and limit interest deductions to the same rate

This option would grant a limited corporate-level dividends paid deduction and conform the treatment of debt to that accorded equity by limiting allowable interest deductions to the same rate. The rate of return could be selected to approximate the rate an investor would demand for a relatively risk-free investment (e.g., the rate on comparable-term Treasury obligations, or a rate several points above that).

The major advantage of this proposal is that the treatment of debt and equity would be more closely aligned since the cost of all externally-raised capital generally would be deductible to the same extent. This could remove some of the importance of distinguishing debt from equity.

In addition, the proposal might alleviate pressure for the issuance of debt, and to this extent would address non-tax issues related to concern about the economic consequences of leverage. This proposal, standing alone, is not designed to address any issues related to the potential erosion of the tax base. Although the deduction with respect to debt would be limited, the new deduction for equity might offset that limit in many cases. Depending upon the rate selected and the transitional rules adopted, the total amount of available deductions might be reduced for some corporations, but might increase for others.

Moreover, the proposal does not address issues related to the reduction of the corporate tax base by debt-financed distributions or by other distributions. However, it could be combined with other proposals directed to such issues.

One issue with respect to this approach is the selection of the appropriate deductible rate. The selection of the effective date of the proposal involves additional issues. For example, granting a dividends paid deduction for capital contributed prior to the effective date of the proposal could arguably provide a windfall for such capital. Similarly, cutting back interest deductions for debt incurred prior to that debt could be viewed as undermining existing expectations.

If the deduction for equity is granted only to "new" capital, rules would have to be provided to prevent the retirement of existing capital and its reissuance as "new" capital eligible for the deduction. The minimum distributions tax proposal described below at Part V.D.1. of this pamphlet, infra, might provide a method of enforcing such a limitation.

Providing a deduction only for "new" capital might also raise questions whether new equity (or new corporations) might obtain some advantage over old equity (and old corporations.) Such concerns might be addressed by allowing the deduction for all capital but phasing it in slowly, or by requiring the deduction for each infusion of new capital to be phased out over some period of time.

2. Allow an investor credit for interest and dividends and deny corporate interest deduction

This option would not permit a corporation to deduct any interest. Instead, shareholders and debtholders would be allowed a credit against taxes owed as a result of their receipt of dividends and interest. The credit would be based, in some fashion, on corporate taxes paid with respect to the dividends and interest distributed by a corporation.

One advantage of this option is that the tax treatment of debt and equity would be equalized. One issue raised by this option is the effect it would have on other business entities (e.g., partnerships), depending on whether the option applied only to corporations or to a broader class of business entities. The other issues raised by this option are similar to those discussed in connection with integration proposals generally (see Part V.A. of this pamphlet, supra.

D. Other Options

1. Impose minimum tax on distributions

A minimum tax could be imposed on certain corporate distributions (for example, extraordinary dividends, stock redemption distributions, and amounts distributed in corporate acquisitions) to assure that the corporate revenue base is not reduced without payment of at least a minimum amount of tax.[172]

One approach would impose the tax at a rate equal to the rate on dividends received by individuals (e.g. 28 percent). The tax could be withheld from the dividend distribution by the distributing corporation and a credit provided to the shareholder against any shareholder tax on the distribution.

This approach directly addresses the issue of the erosion of the corporate base by focusing on the cause of the erosion, i.e., distributions out of corporate solution. The approach recognizes that the erosion can occur whether or not debt is incurred and whether or not an acquisition transaction such as a leveraged buyout is involved. Its application to all major corporate distribution transactions would ensure that a minimum tax would in fact be collected, regardless of the nature of the distributee and of the specific tax characterization of the distribution.

---

[172]. A variation of this approach was suggested by Professor William D. Andrews in a *Reporter's Study on Corporate Distributions*, published as an Appendix to the American Law Institute's *Federal Income Tax Project, Subchapter C, Proposals on Corporate Acquisitions and Dispositions* (1982). The Reporter's Study made three specific proposals relating to the taxation of corporate income. The proposals would (1) provide a deduction for dividends paid on new corporate equity, (2) impose a compensatory tax on nondividend distributions, and (3) modify the tax treatment of intercorporate investment and distributions. The proposals contained in the Reporter's Study have not been adopted by the American Law Institute.

At the shareholder level, any bias in the tax law in favor of non-dividend distributions (treated as sales) as opposed to dividend distributions would be eliminated.

One issue related to this approach is that certain arguably unfair results may occur from the distributee's standpoint because the same tax is withheld from a distribution regardless of a shareholder's basis in the shares. In addition, the proposal would collect tax with respect to certain distributions to tax-exempt investors that are not currently taxed. This effect would be mitigated to the extent that ordinary distributions (such as ordinary dividends) might be exempted from the proposal.

It is arguable that the proposal might subject corporate income to multiple taxation if the corporation is taxed on earnings, a taxable selling shareholder is taxed on gain that is attributable to retained earnings, and the purchasing shareholder is also taxed on the distribution in redemption of his recently-acquired shares. However, such multiple taxation would be mitigated to the extent tax is deferred or eliminated either at the corporate or the shareholder level. For example, the corporation might not pay current tax on corporate earnings or appreciation that may underlie a selling shareholder's gain (because of corporate-level tax deductions that do not reflect economic losses, or because appreciation has not been recognized at the corporate level). Similarly, a selling shareholder may obtain a deferral benefit by not recognizing gain until his stock is sold. Also, such multiple taxation would not occur to the extent that the purchasing shareholder anticipates the new minimum distributions tax (or anticipated a tax on distributions under present law), and accordingly reduced the price paid to the selling shareholder.

2. **Require recognition of corporate-level gain to the extent corporate-level debt is incurred in excess of corporate-level underlying asset basis**

A portion of corporate-level appreciation could be recognized whenever debt is incurred in excess of underlying corporate-level asset basis. This proposal could be limited to situations where the debt supports a distribution out of corporate solution.

Under this approach, the distributing corporation is viewed as having cashed out a portion of its asset appreciation, since it has removed that value from corporate solution rather than using the funds to pay down corporate-level debt supported in part by appreciation in corporate assets. * * * The approach addresses issues related to the erosion of the corporate revenue base and also issues related to the measurement of economic income.

It is arguable that since the corporation is still liable for its debt, it has not obtained any advantage from the borrowing and distribution and should not be required to accelerate recognition of corporate level gain. On the other hand, to the extent corporate asset appreciation supported the borrowing, the funds have been removed from corporate solution, and the remaining corporate assets are the only source of repayment, it is arguable that the benefits of the corporate appreciation have been realized at this point.

3. Impose excise tax on acquisition indebtedness

A nondeductible excise tax at a rate that would approximate denial of a corporate level interest deduction could be imposed in the case of certain distributions where debt is involved. This tax could be designed to parallel any of the interest disallowance proposals described above that address acquisitions or other types of corporate distributions.

To the extent the tax depends upon identification of an amount of indebtedness that supports a particular type of transaction, it will involve the debt allocation issues discussed above in connection with interest disallowance proposals.

To the extent the tax is imposed only on certain types of indebtedness (for example, where the interest rate or the debt-equity ratio exceeds a certain amount), it raises the further issue whether transactions could be structured to avoid the particular limitations while varying other aspects of the transaction to produce similar economic results.

Finally, to the extent the tax is imposed only on certain types of stock purchases (for example, purchases of 50 percent of the stock of a corporation within a specified time), it will be limited in the extent to which it addresses broader questions relating to erosion of the corporate tax base or the proper matching of corporate-level deductions with income.

The principal issue such an excise tax would attempt to address is the potential concern related to interest disallowance proposals that foreign acquirors able to borrow abroad might be advantaged over U.S. acquirors. However, to the extent the excise tax is dependent upon the identification of some amount of debt supporting the acquisition, it may involve administrative issues since it may be difficult to identify the amount of foreign incurred debt supporting a U.S. acquisition. A presumption might be established that all or a specified percentage of a foreign acquiror's purchase price was debt-financed. Possibly foreign acquirors could be given an opportunity to rebut the presumption. However, it might be difficult for the Internal Revenue Service to audit any such rebuttal statements, which could require obtaining information about the entity's foreign capital structure.

4. Develop objective standards for distinguishing between debt and equity

The possibility of issuing Treasury regulations under section 385 could be revisited. Such an approach could attempt to develop more objective standards for distinguishing between debt and equity. Prior attempts to develop such standards have been unsuccessful. * * *

5. Proposals relating to employee stock ownership plans

To the extent that any proposal relating to the deductibility of interest payments in connection with leveraged buyouts is adopted, special consideration should be given to whether similar restrictions should be imposed on employer contributions to ESOPs that are used to repay loans used to acquire employer securities. The availability of the special rules for ESOP-related borrowing arguably would perpetuate an advantage of debt over equity in ESOP situations.

If the special tax incentives for leveraged ESOPS are retained, some would propose a general review of the leveraging rules relating to ESOPs to determine if the rules can be modified to better ensure that employees will benefit significantly from ESOP transactions. They argue that even if the special tax benefits for leveraged ESOPs are appropriate, changes could be made to preserve the incentives to establish ESOPs, but also provide better safeguards for employees. Examples of possible changes are modifications to the voting rules for ESOPs, or a requirement that an employer may not establish an ESOP unless it is supplemental to another tax-qualified retirement plan.

PART THREE: TAXATION OF S CORPORATIONS

CHAPTER 16. THE S CORPORATION

C. ELECTION, REVOCATION AND TERMINATION

Page 713:

After the first full paragraph, add:

In the 1987 Act, Congress relaxed the taxable year requirements by allowing S corporations (along with partnerships and certain personal service corporations) to elect to adopt, retain or change to a fiscal year under certain conditions, including the payment of an entity-level tax.

Section 444 permits a newly formed S corporation to elect to use a taxable year other than the calendar year required by Section 1378 provided that the year elected results in no more than a three-month deferral of income to the shareholders.[29] S corporations formed or electing S status prior to the enactment of the 1987 Act may elect to retain a taxable year that is the same as the entity's last taxable year beginning in 1986.[30] This special election (which may result in a deferral period of more than three months) is available only if it is made for the entity's first taxable year beginning after December 31, 1986.[31] In any other case where an S corporation wishes to change a taxable year, a Section 444 election may be made only if the resulting deferral of income to the shareholders is not more than the shorter of three months or the deferral period of the taxable year being changed.[32] § 444(b)(2).

An S corporation that elects a fiscal year under Section 444 must make a "required payment" under Section 7519 for any taxable year for which the election is in effect. The mechanics of the required payment are annoyingly complex, but the concept is clear enough. An electing S corporation must pay (and keep "on deposit") an amount roughly approximating the value of the tax deferral that the shareholders would have achieved if a Section 444 election had not been made. Thus, if an S corporation whose shareholders all used calendar years elected a fiscal year ending September 30, the corporation would be required to pay a tax that supposedly equalled the tax benefit from the

---

29. I.R.C. § 444(a), (b)(1).
30. I.R.C. § 444(b)(3).
31. Id.
32. I.R.C. § 444(b)(2).

three months' deferral received by the shareholders.[33] Under a de minimis rule, no payment is required if the amount due is less than $500,[34] and a payment made in one year generates a balance "on deposit" which may be used in subsequent years).[35] As a transitional measure, the entity-level payment requirement is phased in over several years through an "applicable percentage" (25 percent in 1987; 50 percent in 1988; 75 percent in 1989; and 100 percent in 1990 and thereafter) mechanism.[36]

A Section 444 election and Section 7519 required payment are not required for any S corporation that has established a business purpose for a fiscal year under Section 1378(b)(2).[37]

D. TREATMENT OF THE SHAREHOLDERS

Page 717:

After the *Selfe* case, add:

NOTE

Declining to follow the Eleventh Circuit's decision in *Selfe*, the Tax Court held in Estate of Leavitt v. Commissioner, 90 T.C. 206 (1988) that the guarantee of an S corporation's bank loan by several shareholders could not be treated as an additional investment in the corporation and did not increase the shareholders' bases for purposes of the loss limitations in the pre-1983 version of Section 1366. The court reasoned that a basis increase was not permitted without an actual economic outlay by the shareholder. It refused to accept the taxpayer's argument that, in substance, the transaction was a loan from the bank to the shareholder-guarantors, who then advanced the loan proceeds to the corporation as a contribution to capital. In so holding, the court declined to apply debt-equity principles used under Subchapter C.

In a lengthy dissent, Judge Fay concluded that: (1) debt-equity principles under Subchapter C are applicable in determining whether a shareholder-guaranteed corporate debt should be characterized as a capital contribution; and (2) applying such principles, the shareholders in *Leavitt* should be considered as having made a contribution to capital because the bank looked solely to them for repayment of the loan.

33. We say "supposedly" because the Section 7519 "required payment" is determined mechanically, without regard to amounts actually deferred by the shareholders. See § 7519(b), (c), (d) for the details.

34. I.R.C. § 7519(a)(2).

35. I.R.C. § 7519(b)(2).

36. I.R.C. § 7519(d)(4).

37. I.R.S. Notice 88–10, 1988-1 C.B. 478.

The Tax Court's decision has been affirmed by the Fourth Circuit (89-1 U.S.T.C. ¶ 9332 (May 19, 1989)), creating a conflict in the circuits and possibly setting the stage for Supreme Court review of this issue.

E. DISTRIBUTIONS TO SHAREHOLDERS

Page 722:

Add to footnote 10:

TAMRA repealed Sections 1363(d) and (e) as deadwood. These provisions were unnecessary in light of Section 1371(a), which provides that, except as otherwise provided in Subchapter S, the provisions of Subchapter C apply to S corporations and their shareholders. Thus, Sections 311 and 336 govern the extent to which an S corporation recognizes gain or loss on a distribution of property with respect to its stock. In general, this means that the gain recognition rule formerly in Section 1363(d) lives on in Section 311(b) (for nonliquidating distributions) and Section 336(a) (for liquidating distributions).

F. TAXATION OF THE S CORPORATION

Pages 726–727:

Delete the first full paragraph on page 726 through the carryover paragraph on page 727 and insert:

To deter this tax avoidance technique, Congress enacted Section 1374, which taxes an S corporation that has a "net recognized built-in gain" at any time within ten years of the effective date of its S corporation election.[5] At the outset, two important limitations on this tax should be noted. First, Section 1374 applies only if the corporation's S election was made after December 31, 1986.[6] Second, it does not apply to a corporation which always has been an S corporation.[7]

In general, Section 1374 is designed to tax S corporations on the net gain that accrued while the corporation was subject to Subchapter C if that gain is subsequently recognized on sales, distributions and other dispositions of property within a "recognition period" which is the ten year period beginning with the first taxable year for which the corporation was an S corporation. For this purpose, any gain recognized during the recognition period is a "recognized built-in gain" unless the corporation establishes either that it did not hold the asset at the beginning of its first S corporation taxable year or the recognized gain

---

5. I.R.C. §§ 1374(a), (d)(7). As indicated in the deleted portions of the main text, the tax operated somewhat differently as originally enacted in the 1986 Act but was modified in 1988 by TAMRA.

6. Tax Reform Act of 1986, P.L. No. 99–514, 99th Cong., 2d Sess. § 633(b) (1986).

7. I.R.C. § 1374(c)(1). This exemption may not apply, however, if the S corporation had a "predecessor" that was a C corporation. Id. (last sentence). This could occur, for example, where a C corporation was acquired by the S corporation in a tax-free reorganization.

exceeds the gain inherent in the asset at that time.[8] Conversely, any loss recognized during the recognition period is a "recognized built-in loss" to the extent that the S corporation establishes that it held the asset at the beginning of its first "S year" and the loss does not exceed the loss which was inherent in the asset at that time.[9] Since the burden of proof under these definitions falls on the taxpayer, a corporation making an S election after 1986 is well advised to obtain an independent appraisal of its assets to establish their value on the relevant date in order to avoid being taxed on gain arising under the "S" regime and to take into account losses that accrued during the corporation's "C" years.

Turning to the precise workings of the statute, the Section 1374 tax is computed by applying the highest tax rate applicable to C corporations (currently, 34 percent) to the S corporation's "net recognized built-in gain", which is defined as the corporation's taxable income computed by taking into account only recognized built-in gains and losses, but limited to the corporation's taxable income computed generally as if it were a C corporation.[10] The purpose of the taxable income limitation is to ensure that Section 1374 does not tax the corporation on more income than it actually realizes during the taxable year. To prevent taxpayers from manipulating the timing of post-conversion losses, however, TAMRA added Section 1374(d)(2)(B), which provides that any net recognized built-in gain not taxed because of the taxable income limitation will be carried forward and subjected to tax in succeeding years in the recognition period. Finally, in all events the amount of net recognized built-in gain taken into account for any taxable year may not exceed the net unrealized built-in gain at the time the corporation became an S corporation reduced by any net recognized built-in gains which were subject to Section 1374 in prior taxable years.[11]

As originally enacted in the 1986 Act, the Section 1374 tax literally applied only to built-in gains recognized on the disposition of an asset that was held by the S corporation at the beginning of the first taxable year for which an S election was in effect. Assume, however, that a C corporation converting to S status holds an asset (Oldacre) with a built-in gain which it subsequently exchanges for property of like kind (Newacre) in a Section 1031 nonrecognition transaction. The gain

---

8. I.R.C. § 1374(d)(3).
9. I.R.C. § 1374(d)(4).
10. I.R.C. § 1374(b)(1), (d)(2). Taxable income, as defined in Section 63(a), is modified by disregarding certain deductions (e.g., the dividends received deduction) and net operating losses under Section 172.

I.R.C. §§ 1374(d)(2)(A)(ii); 1375(b)(1)(B). Net operating loss and capital loss carryforwards from prior years as a C corporation, are taken into account in computing the amount subject to tax under Section 1374. I.R.C. § 1374(b)(2).

11. I.R.C. § 1374(c)(2), (d)(1).

inherent in Oldacre will be preserved in Newacre's exchanged basis under Section 1031(d) and, if the corporation disposes of Newacre within ten years after switching to S status, the Section 1374 tax logically should apply to the built-in "C gain" even though Newacre was not held by the corporation when it became an S corporation.

TAMRA closed this statutory gap by adding Section 1374(d)(6), which provides that an asset taking an exchanged basis from another asset held by the S corporation at the time it converted to "S" status shall be treated as having been held by the S corporation as of the beginning of its first S year. Returning to the above example, the built-in gain inherent in Oldacre at the time the corporation converted to S status will be recognized under Section 1374 if the corporation recognizes a gain on disposition of Newacre during the recognition period. TAMRA also added Section 1374(d)(8), a similar provision designed to ensure that built-in gain in assets acquired by an S corporation from a C corporation in a tax-free reorganization does not escape the Section 1374 tax. For this purpose, however, Section 1374(d)(8)(B) provides that the recognition period commences as of the date the asset is acquired rather than on the beginning of the first taxable year for which the corporation was an S corporation. For an illustration of the gambits at which these anti-avoidance provisions are directed, see Problem 1(d) at page 732 of the main volume and Problem 3 at page 735.

†